VISITOR'S GUIDE

ROYAL PALACE
OF MADRID

José Luis Sancho

© EDITORIAL PATRIMONIO NACIONAL. 1996
   Palacio Real de Madrid
   Bailén, s/n
   28071 MADRID
   Tel. 559.74.04
© ALDEASA. 1996
© of all texts from José Luis Sancho Gaspar

N.I.P.O. 006-96-010-1

Depósito Legal: M-29755-1996
I.S.B.N. 84-7120-198-4
I.S.B.N. 84-8003-071-2

Design and Layout: Alberto Caffaratto
Translation: Alicia Lewin
Photographs: Patrimonio Nacional, Félix Lorrio, Ramón Guerra, Antonio Sanz

Photomechanical: Lucam

Cover Illustration: View of the main facade of the Madrid Royal Palace, from the *Lithographic Collection of Views of Royal Manors,* by Fernando Brambilla, 1832.
Printed by: TF. Madrid

Printed in Spain.

CONTENTS

INTRODUCTION

FROM FORTRESS TO PALACE.

The Royal Palace stands at the very place where the Madrid citadel "famous castle" used to be, built at the end of the IXth century, during the cordovan emirate of Mohammed I, as a key position for the defense of the territory north of Toledo.

The fortress, rebuilt in the XIVth century, acquired the condition of a royal residence with the construction performed under Juan II, excelling among them the chapel, consecrated in 1434, and the large "rich hall". It was already in the XVIth century when Carlos V and Felipe II rebuilt it as a Royal Palace, so that since 1561 the Alcazar became the permanent residence of the Kings, so that Madrid, a village emerged under the protection of its castle became the Court of the Spanish Monarchy. Under Felipe IV, the Palace acquired its most characteristic shape: on the outside, the large façade designed by Francisco and Juan Gómez de Mora and G. B. Crescenci; on the inside, with the participation of Diego Velázquez as interior designer architect and with the display of masterpieces that nowadays are gems of the Prado Museum. Felipe V also left his trace at the Alcazar before the greatest and best part of its structure disappeared on a fire on the Christmas eve of 1734.

The location of the Alcazar and its arrangement, conceived around the buildings lodging the living quarters, did condition in such a way the shape of the New Royal Palace and its environment that we could almost state that even today it is still present, in spite of the disappearance of all visible remains in the area.

The Royal Manors

The fact that Madrid, and more accurately the Alcazar or Royal Palace, would constitute the seat of the power did not preclude the possibility for the King to dwell in other places. The game preserves near Madrid utilized by the Trastamaras - El Pardo, Valsaín -, the country estate in Aranjuez incorporated into the Crown by the Catholic Monarchs, the Monastery of El Escorial, built under Felipe II, and other properties also founded by the latter Monarch - mainly the neighboring Casa de Campo, at the other side of the Manzanares - constituted a system of "Royal Manors" that was defined at the time the capital city was here established, and that through the three following centuries was enlarged and improved with new Sites like the Buen Retiro or the Granja de San Ildefonso, creations of Felipe IV and Felipe V respectively: The use of these residences was seasonal according to their nature and qualities: springtime was spent at Aranjuez, summer at Valsaín -since Felipe V at the nearby La Granja -, autumn at El Escorial... The Monarchs stayed in Madrid from the end of October on

The Palace in the city.
"The palace itself stands in one of the few fine situations the city affords; being placed on a considerable eminence, overlooking the least uninteresting side of the country ..."
ANONYMOUS: *Spain, Tangier, etc. visited in 1840 and 1841*. By X.Y.Z., London, 1845.

"The palace is a noble building of white stone, occupying a commanding situation, and looks very imposing from a distance."
Louisa Mary Anne TENISON: *Castile and Andalucia*. London, 1853

"This is certainly one of the most magnificent royal residences in the world, imposing in itself, and striking from its position at the end of the finest part of the town, on the edge of a steep bank."
Augustus John Cuthbert HARE: *Wanderings in Spain*, London, 1873.

The Western façade of the Palace, towards the river, from the Park or Campo del Moro.

The Alcazar in Felipe II's day. Detail of a picture by Alonso Sánchez Coello. Monastery of the Descalzas Reales. Madrid.

Juvarra and his plan.

"It is said that minister Campillo, to support his political or economic objectives, or both; impeded that Don Filippo Juvarra's great plan be performed, an enterprise considered capable to empty even the funds of the Spanish Monarch. Ideas so extremely vast as master Filippo used to get out from his not less vast mind, to whom, once outlined in a piece of paper, they cost him of course less than what it would mean to other people once they were built on a site".
P. Norberto CAIMO (the Italian Idler). *Voyage d'Espagne, fait en l'année 1755...* Paris, 1772-1773

"A mahogany model of the projected palace is still shown in Madrid, and must of itself have cost the price of as good a dwelling as any modest man need wish for. This palace was to have lodged the royal body guard, the ministers, tribunals, and indeed every thing connected with the machine of state"
Alexander Sidell MACKENZIE: *A year in Spain, by a young American.* London, 1831.

Detail of the main façade of Juvarra's plan for the Madrid Royal Palace.A.G.P.

until the Holy Week, but with prolonged stays at the winter hunting place: El Pardo. Felipe V and, mainly, Carlos III took to the extreme this systematic absence from the capital. This criterion did not work always in a strict way, but although it were subject to exceptions, novelties and changes imposed by the liking of each Monarch, the fact is that it ruled for three centuries the life in the Spanish Court, the axis of which remained being the Palace of Madrid.

The New Royal Palace

Just upon the fire of that Christmas Eve of 1734 was out, Felipe V decided to build a new Royal Palace in Madrid, and to do it at the very same place as the former one, symbolizing the continuity of the Monarchy. He wanted the entire structure to be vault, using timber strictly for doors and windows, in order to avoid another fire, and perhaps also with the desire of identifying the firmness of the seat with that of power: the inscription in the foundation stone claims that it was built "to eternity". The Palace had to house all the duties of the Court, one of the most important in Europe at that time, moreover in a moment in which the idea regarding the splendor that should surround the regal power was reaching its highest quota.

THE ARCHITECTURE: DESIGN AND CONSTRUCTION.

Felipe V also wanted the architect of his Palace to be the top one in Europe, and he made the right choice. At the beginning of 1735, the Italian Filippo Juvarra who had been invited to Madrid, quickly realized that the location of the Alcazar was not appropriate for a residence as large and magnificent as conceived, and consequently he thought up an extremely huge project of a horizontal development, much more suitable for a flat place. However, since Juvarra died in March 1736 the Monarchs, that were delighted with his style, decided to call a disciple of his to build the master's great project.

Thus G. B. Sacchetti, who hailed from Turin, came to Madrid, and was commissioned a very difficult matter: to "adapt" Juvarra's design to the site of the original Palace; but since G.B. did not have neither Juvarra's prestige nor his personality, he could not afford to object and so he obeyed.

The final shape of the Palace is the result of a complicated process, the fundamental points of which are Juvarra's drawings; the adaptation of his schemes, that actually is a totally new project of Sacchetti, modified, in turn, in many aspects during its construction; and further by the modifications that Sacchetti's Palace underwent due to Sabatini, Carlos III's architect.

The architectural design of the Palace, in its general features and its details, is characteristic of Juavarra's classicist late baroque taste,

View of the Royal Palace from the "Calle Nueva". Fernando Brambilla.

Partial view of Madrid including the Royal Palace and the river. Fernando Brambilla

Fachada Principal del Proyecto de Dⁿ Felipe Juvarra, para el Real Palacio de Madrid.

Plan for the Madrid Royal Palace, main façade towards the city. Filippo Javarra. 1735.

Main façade. Detail.

very much inspired by Bernini, a famous Roman artist, and it follows the lines of the unaccomplished great project. But the originally conceived horizontality had to be turned by Sacchetti into verticality in order that, taking up the same lot of the old palace, the New Palace be able to lodge the royal people, the courtiers, the staff, the ministries and the auxiliary outbuildings, thus the building has a minimum of six storeys and a maximum of eight: two basements that span the ground unevenness by the West and the North, for the "offices of home and mouth" and for the dispatching secretariats. Summer and winter rooms,respectively, in the first and second floors, meant for the royal people. The third floor for the ladies and the gentlemen at their service. And finally, the rooms in the mezzanines that are over the first, second and third floors, for the staff.

The general ground floor of the building did not change since the first plan, dated March 9, 1737; square, with only one main courtyard, also square, in the center and surrounded by galleries with arcades. The main rooms are arranged in line along the façades, the antechambers and the secondary rooms look at the courtyard, and along the space between the two walls run service corridors. Three small courtyards are used to give light to the interior rooms of the angles. Something of the spirit of the Alcazar seems to float around the New Palace, since its obvious solidity, the projections or "towers" at the corners, the escarpment at the lower part of its walls, its elevation and its situation, endow it an air of a fortress.

Between 1738 and 1747, while the works were progressing, Sacchetti made some changes in his plan as a result of the criticisms of the Queen's secretary, the Marquis Annibale Scotti, and of some architects linked to the work. In 1742, and due to Scotti's influence, he gave a greater development to the staircase turning it into two, twin and symmetrical; and in between he left a hall for social gatherings - the current Halberdiers Room - where according to his first ideas the Chapel was supposed to be located, which was moved to the Northern side, thereby harmonizing the Alcazar reminiscences, Sacchetti's obsession for symmetry and the urge for ostentation of the Spanish Monarchs, who in those days wanted the Court spaces to be with the greatest possible magnificence.

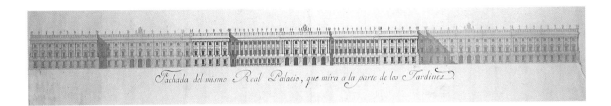

Fachada del mismo Real Palacio, que mira a la parte de los Jardines

THE PALACE DWELLERS AND THE DECORATIVE CHANGES.

The inner distribution and the decoration are two aspects closely linked in a residence, and they usually change simultaneously, according to the needs and tastes of the succeeding generations of occupants. Each reign implies different people and likings and, moreover, the idea about how the representation of the royal Majesty had to be like was evolving along with the social and political changes: there is a chasm between the personal significance of the King in an

Plan for the Madrid Royal Palace, façade towards the gardens. Filippo Juavarra, 1735

Eastern façade.

Sacchetti.

"The Royal Palace is being built with a great magnificence, and with an even greater cost. Five million pesos have been already spent and four thousand workers have been working at the same time, although currently there are no more than one thousand and they work slowly... However, it can not be denied that this is a superb, grandiose mass, accompanied by anything that can make it look beautiful, ornamented, comfortable and fitting enough to the majesty of a Sovereign. To carry it out this way, the Turinese Sacchetti has furnished all his talent and he would have given more if he had have more of it; but still he has not been able to please the majority of those that have eyes. Among them some do not approve the abundance of basements, which, if I am not mistaken, reach the number of seven; some in turn think the eleven spans are overly excessive, and more, that have the thickness of the main walls, since it is not the case of a blockhouse; some pedale do not consider the staircase to be acceptable due to its roughness and inconvenience; some criticize the courtyards, others do the rooms, the windows, or, finally, the great expenses and the workers' indolence; and to me of course the latter deserve the most stern criticisms. Even my footman, who has worked before for an architect believes he is his disciple, wanted to come out with his miserable critical opinion. I believe it is unquestionable that had he performed the magnificent model of abbé Juvarra, whose model can still be seen at the Retiro, would have had also his correctors". P. Norberto CAIMO: *Voyage d'Espagne, fait en l'année 1755... Paris, 1772.*

Absolute Monarchy, its transformation under Liberalism in the XIXth century and eventually in parliamentary democracy.

The plans in the back flap speak for themselves regarding the arrangement in each reign. Fernando VI did not think about children he did not have, and thus his Room and the Queen's one turned out to be almost as large as required by the idea that their contemporaries had about a regal residence. Conversely, Carlos III had to have the halls divided and still, the Palace was always small for him, as to his son. In the eyes of the following generations it seemed larger and larger, even excessive, because the ideas had been changing.

The decorations conceived under Fernando VI by Sacchetti, Giaquinto and other artists were of a late baroque style rather overelaborated, but they were also modified with the arrival of Carlos III, who brought along a relatively more sober and classicist taste, whose artificer was the Sicilian Francisco Sabatini, a disciple and son-in-law of the architect of the Palace of Caserta, Luigi Vanvitelli. Sabatini directed all the aspects of the inner decoration of the Palace, except when the King's will was to commission it to somebody else - such as in the Throne Hall or in the rooms carried out by Gasparini -, and he did it by harmonizing the dignity of the design with the richness of the materials: the magnificent marbles of the jambs and baseboards, all of them Spanish, of which were gathered in the Palace a collection of samples including over three hundred types; the solid mahogany of all the passage doors, windows and shutters. Sabatini and his team performed the designs of the stuccoes, the carving of the furniture, and the ornamental bronzes - the latter are missing for the most part -, carried out by several Italian and French masters chosen and recruited by him. During the almost forty years of his activity at the Palace, from 1760 to 1797, his liking and that of his patrons was evolving from the fondness to the rococo to the classicist shapes.

Along with Sabatini, the artist who most deeply marked the decoration of the New Palace was the painter Anton Raphael Mengs and not only because he performed here some his masterpieces, but also because the high esteem nourished for him by the King turned him into an artistic dictator, who in order to decorate the remaining vaults freely chose young Spanish painters and imprinted in them his personal style: Francisco Bayeu and Mariano Salvador Maella were the more prominent, in detriment of Corrado Giaquinto's disciples, an almighty individual at the Palace under Fernando VI and an author of very beautiful frescoes.

Under Carlos III and Carlos IV a fundamental element in the decoration were the pictures that totally covered the walls from the frieze or baseboard to the cornice: the visitors remained perplexed before the combination of such an accumulation of masterpieces and the ornamental sumptuousness of the Palace. In some rooms tapestries would substitute the paintings during the wintertime. However at the

beginning of the XIXth century the taste changed: one single picture on the wall was enough, at the most, on top of the silk hanging or of the wallpapers that began to be used by then. Thus Fernando VII relegated the great majority of the masterpieces that later on he gathered at the Royal Gallery of Painting, currently the Prado Museum.

The look of the halls is also definitely "Fernando VII" or "Fernandino" style due to other essential furniture elements. Carlos IV had a passion for French furniture and decorative objects, so that the Royal collections keep splendid pieces of that period. This fondness was continued by his son Fernando VII who, mainly between 1818 and 1830, carried out massive acquisitions of Parisian bronze objects: clocks, candelabra and chandeliers. In spite of their beauty, they are so numerous that it is not possible to expand on the description of each one of them: when no more details are given, it means they are "Fernandino style" and from Paris. The effect of a profuse richness "Empire" style that they caused had to be tremendous then, when they were concentrated on the western half side of the Palace, deeper than now that are dispersed all over the residence.

Northern façade of the Palace, with the dome of the Royal Chapel, from the Sabatini gardens.

Gilded and chiselled bronze chandelier. A XIXth century french job.

Audiences and visits in the Ancien Régime.
"His Majesty grants audience some given days of the week. Those who wish to have the honor and kiss his hand, to mention him any matter or to submit to him an application, obtain said permission by addressing a note, to the captain of the royal guard, in the morning till nine a.m., who, if pertinent, sets the time in which the applicant may expound it: in order to talk to the Princes it is necessary to follow the same steps..." "The richness and beauties that this Palace contains are countless...The caretaker or chief lodger who lives at the very Palace furnishes the exhibition of all these curiosities while Their Majesties are absent".
A walk in Madrid or the Court Visitor's guide. Madrid, 1815.

Main façade of the Palace and Parade Square.

The "King tower" with the Moctezuma statue, in the main façade of the Palace.

Isabel II's ornamental changes, although being important on the eastern half of the building, and mainly in her private rooms, are insignificant compared to those of both her father and her son, Alfonso XII. The Restoration brought a desire for updating the Madrid Palace according to the parameters of the Victorian royal residences, within the taste of the conservative bourgeoisie of the end of the XIXth century for multicolored and obscure interiors. The works were directed by the architect José Segundo de Lema and they consisted in revamping and decorating a ball and formal dinner room and other annexes, a billiards room, a smoking room, and the parquet laying in many of the private rooms and of the halls, which besides were furnished pursuant to the style of the time. For that purpose some very important decorations and frescoes from Mengs were sacrificed. The XXth century has been marked by the great restoration works performed after the last Spanish Civil War of 1936-1939, and by those of the last years.

THE VISIT

THE PARADE SQUARE AND THE MAIN FAÇADE.

The access to the Royal Palace from the city has been always via "calle Mayor" (main street) up to the *Royal Armory*. This building, that was demolished in 1884 and that has given name to the existing Square between the cathedral of La Almudena and the Palace, was approximately located where there is now the large iron gate of access.

After going across the iron gate the *Palace Square* is reached, also called *the Armory Square*, since the Military Parade and the ordinance honors take place there, that since the XVIth century has been the scenery where the Court's pomp would go out to appear before the people, with the main façade of the royal residence as a backcloth. Sacchetti and Ventura Rodríguez conceived this Square with open porticos that would connect the Palace with the service buildings, but Sabatini assigned to this space its current character of *"cour d'honneur"* in the French way, enclosed by two prolongations of the royal rooms, of which only was finished the one on the right side called *St. Gil Wing* in 1783 and its decoration in 1788. The left hand wing never did exceed the level of the second floor.

The low pavilions that constitute the sides of the Square follow the general outlines drawn by Sabatini, but they are already from the XIXth century and they correspond, like the railing, to the project of Narciso Pascual y Colomer (1847), who under Isabel II's reign finished that of the right hand side; the one on the left was performed between 1883 and 1893 by his successors. The arches opened at the

Parade Square, with the Royal Guard on Parade.

Royal Palace. North-west angle.

15

The Parade Square.

"...One (of the really beautiful landscapes that have impressed him) is the view from the terrace of the Royal Palace. Crossing the Parade Square, where every morning takes place the Military Parade, one goes under the gallery that at the Western side is the limit of the Palace and of the city, and, among the white pillars supporting the arches, a whole green, deep valley, is framed, that like a garden waterfall and trees descends step by step down to the Manzanares river going up again at the other side, where the hills and forests spread out towards the rocky top mountains. The lines are very noble with a very interesting general tone: it helps to understand Velázquez' pictures, their immense remoteness of a sad green that borders with a shineless blue".
René BAZIN: *Terre d'Espagne*. Paris, 1905.

Relief of The Spanish arms. Gian Domenico Oliveri.

left side over the Palace Park allow to understand the fascination that this location inspired. At the other side of the river, the Casa de Campo spreads out as far as connecting with El Pardo Woodlands and, at the remoteness of the sierra, in the clear days it is possible to see the Monastery of El Escorial. The continuity of all those royal properties was even more pronounced while the La Florida, also called La Moncloa, Royal Country House, created by Carlos IV was still existing; it occupied an area including what nowadays is the Argüelles quarter, plus the Western Park and the University Campus.

The shapes of the architecture of the Palace, inspired in Bernini and Juvarra can be observed in detail on the *main façade*. Over a bossed base, that corresponds to the ground or first floor and to the first mezzanine, raises a gigantic order of pilasters and columns that articulate the main floor, mezzanine and third floor; the large general cornice is crowned by a balustrade that hides the lead roofs.

The great number of statues performed by a numerous team of Spanish artists led by the Italian Gian Domenico Olivieri and by the Galician Felipe de Castro, main sculptors of Fernando VI, gave to the building a great baroque plasticity and propagandistic sense. The statues placed over the crowning balustrade represented the Kings of Spain, starting with the first of the Goth Kings to and including Fernando VI; while at the level of the main floor, over the pedestals at the angles, there were, by couples, "suevo" kings, counts of Castile, kings of Navarre, Aragon and Portugal, pre-Columbian emperors and two patron saints of Spain. This sculptural exuberance even increased during the work process, due to the influence of the learned Benedictine Friar Martín Sarmiento, in charge of arranging the complex iconographic program, but it was abruptly suppressed by Carlos III who, to endow the building with a more classicist look, ordered to take all of them away. Only with the modern restoration of the façades, ended in 1973, the statues that can be seen today were replaced. Among the most noteworthy are, at the angles, at the main floor level, the one of *Moctezuma,* emperor of Mexico, by Juan Pascual de Mena (left), and *Atahualpa's* from Peru, by Domingo Martínez.

Where Sabatini placed the four Doric columns, that allowed him to give more projection to the balcony, Fernando VI ordered to install the sculptures of four Roman emperors born in Hispania: *Honorious* and *Teodosius*, by Oliveri, and *Trajan* and *Arcadius* by Castro; they are at the main courtyard since 1791. Above the balcony, which three arch shaped large window spaces were also reduced by Sabatini, the relief of the *Arms of Spain*, it due to Olivieri.

At the attic, the clock was performed according to a design of Sabatini in 1761, year shown in one of the two bells. The other bell that comes from the old clock of the Alcazar is dated in 1637. When the sphere was placed, Sabatini removed the castle in relief, the

Main staircase.

sculpture of the lion with the two worlds and the columns of the *Plus Ultra*, that with the Zodiac - still subsisting at the sides - composed the heraldic emblem of the Crown. In the adjoining pedestals the sculptures of the Kings who built the Palace have been put back.

THE VESTIBULE AND THE MAIN STAIRCASE.

There are five doors at the façade: the vehicles enter to the small vestibules through the two lateral ones and from there to the main courtyard. By the three central gates, to the main vestibule or *portico*, where the columns of Tuscan order, of Sepúlveda pink limestone, keep warm the whiteness of the Colmenar stone. The carriages getting in here leave their occupants - solely Monarchs, Heads of State or Ambassadors - at the foot of the main staircase, at the right-hand side, in front of which Carlos III's statue, by the sculptor Pedro Michel stands up.

As for the staircase, Sacchetti conceived two grandiose twin equally facing each other slopes, that were serving to gain the King's Room at the right-hand side, while the Queen's Room was at the left-

When the Monarchs were leaving the Palace. "On the right hand is the grand staircase: it was lined with battle-axe guards... In the passage there were two or three military men in undress, and seven or eight old women, who were waiting to present memorials to the king; though they could scarcely being ignorant that the time for asking favours from the King of Spain was passed. After waiting some time, the King and Queen descended the staircase, attended by several officiers of state, in full dress: dark blue coats, turned up with crimson, laced with gold ... white smallclothes, and white silk stockings." Michael Joseph QUINN: *A visit to Spain in the latter part of 1822 and the first months of 1823.*

Main staircase. Vault decorated by Corrado Giaquinto.

The two twin main staircases, that of the right-hand side for the King, and the one on the left for the Queen, were an idea of the Marquis Scotti, accepted in 1742. Sacchetti conceived them with a great magnificence and scenographic display, but he stumbled over the criticisms of Scotti himself and of his protégé Bonavia, who felt the steps to be too high. The obsession of performing the ascent as comfortable as possible motivated a court controversy that gave rise to several plans, among which stand out those of Bonavia, the one of the important Roman architects Vanvitelli, Fuga and Salvi, and the alternative plans that Sacchetti himself proposed along those years, taking more and more space towards the Eastern and Western façades.

Bonavia was the first one in proposing a diaphanous staircase well, without intermediate supports, an approach in which he was followed by Sacchetti and the architects of the Roman San Luca Academy, from which advise was sought in 1746. Fuga, Salvi and Vanvitelli, approving Sacchetti, sent, however, a beautiful plan as an ideal solution, but since the Monarchs did not like it, the dispute had to be solved at the end of 1746 by the managing body of the new Academy of Fine Arts of San Fernando. Sacchetti was the winner with his more ambitious plan, and during the following years carried out these two spaces that currently are the main staircase and the Columns Hall; but the ramps, which ingenious and theatrical layout offered nine exits in the main floor, were only built of wood in order to allow the King to see the effect: Carlos III did not like it.

hand side. The two stairwells were built according to his plan and nowadays they are respectively the staircase and the Columns Room.

However, Carlos III did not like neither the shape given by Sacchetti to the ramps nor the layout of the antechambers to enter into his and to the Queen's Room, and reminiscing the staircase of the great palace of

The vault of the main staircase: The Religion protected by Spain, Corrado Giaquinto.

Caserta, built in Naples by Vanvitelli, he had Sabatini build a similar single one in one of the two stairwells leaving the other as a ballroom.

Thus, Sabatini in 1760 made the staircase like it is today, but at the opposite side, i.e. the left-hand side. When Carlos IV acceded to the throne in 1789 he ordered the same architect to move it to the right-hand side, as it is now, for arrangement reasons already commented. Sabatini refurbished the same materials and steps. These consist ofa single piece of San Agustin marble, very low and wide, so that ascending becomes extremely smooth, which was important mainly for the sedan chairs used by the ladies to get to the main floor.

The central flight ends in a large landing, where it is advisable to get near the wall in order to watch the entire space: the lions belong to two different sculptors, with less motion that of the Galician Felipe de Castro, and with more ease the one of Roberto Michel, that gracefully turns his head.

Plan for the main staircase. G.B. Sacchetti, 1745. A.G.P.

Isabel of Farnese. René Fremin.

All the vault decoration, ended in Fernando VI's lifetime, is due to Corrado Giaquinto, over whose designs J.B. Andreoli made the stuccoes. The frescoes are Giaquinto's second work at the Palace, after those of the Chapel and, inasmuch as they were performed while Sacchetti's plan for the staircase was still in force, they are designed to be seen from what was by then the main exit, the tribune called *Camón*, where the sitting statue of *Carlos IV clad as a Roman emperor* is now located.

Therefore it is important to get close to the wall in order to watch the central allegory that represents *The Religion protected by Spain*, while as going up by the second ramps we can contemplate the beautiful personifications of the Abundance, the Peace (at the left-hand side) the Justice and Magnificence (at the right-hand side), in which the contemporaries recognized the characteristic virtues of Fernando VI's reign. *Hercules placing the columns in Gibraltar* at the Camon, above the entrance that Sacchetti arranged as the King's Room, and above the door of the Halberdiers Room *The triumph of Spain over the Saracen power*, along with other small medaillons, complete the pictorial group.

It is a must to evoke here two anecdotes: one about Napoleon, who in his visit to Madrid stopped at the landing and turning his head to the brand-new king Joseph, told him: "Brother, you are going to have a much better home than mine"; the other anecdote is the famous "Battle at the Palace staircase", the attempted kidnapping of child queen Isabel II by General Diego de León and his soldiers, to whom the halberdiers stood up, at the orders of Colonel Dulce (1841).

At the landing of the staircase there are two other important sculptural portraits of Spanish kings from the Bourbon Dynasty, coming from the La Granja Palace: *Felipe V* and his second wife *Isabel of Farnese*, by René Fremin, who also designed the splendid marble and bronze pedestals.

KING CARLOS III'S ROOM

Halberdiers Room

Sacchetti envisaged it as a hall for dances and parties, with several tribunes at the windows level to set the musicians; but Carlos III assigned it for the guards hall, consequently Sabatini decorated it in the simplest possible way with Tuscan pilasters, in lieu of the rich ornamentation that it otherwise would have born. The Colmenar stone and El Molar red stone flooring is likewise of 1760; the flagstones were originally meant for the flooring of the gallery that in this storey surrounds the courtyard; similar is the one of the Antechamber, that is not visible since it is covered by the carpet.

The Guard.
"The Court in Spain used an absolutely extraordinary etiquette and grandeur ... The service of the bodyguard troops included, as it did in all the countries where it existed at that time, such as France, Naples and Spain, mounting guard inside the Royal Palaces, and escorting the Sovereign, both going on foot and on horseback, wherever he went. The Royal Spanish Family demanded by then a considerable service... The King used to go out very often, he would take every day long walks by car with escort, and he would spend the evening in the small palace of El Pardo, near Madrid. For this purpose the escorts were necessary, and he had them in spite of the weather".
Barón de NERVO: *Souvenirs de ma vie...*Paris, 1871.

Vault of the Halberdiers Hall, Venus commending Vulcan to forge the arms for Aeneas, Giambattista Tiépolo.

Felipe V. René Fremin.

But this noble simplicity did not prevent to display the pictorial richness in the fresco, where G.B. Tiépolo performed one of his masterpieces, *Venus commending Vulcan to forge weapons for Aeneas*, a topic inspired in a passage from Virgil's *Aened* and chosen for the military function of the place, although it seems to allude also

Vault of the Columns Hall, The Sun gives life to the forces of Nature. Corrado Giaquinto.

"At the foot of the stairs I shall leave all my spleen, and prepare myself with unfeigned satisfaction to describe to you the beauty and grandeur of the upper apartments. I know no palace in Europe fitted up with so much true royal magnificence."
Henry SWIMBURNE: *Travels through Spain in the years 1775 and 1776.*. London, 1779.

Halberdiers Hall, detail of a mahogany and bronze console table according to Francisco Sabatini's designs, 1791.

to Carlos III, as a warrior hero, and to his mother Queen Isabel of Farnese, as the promoter of his Italian conquests.

The furniture of this room was very simple until the XXth century; limited to benches and other objects for the halberdiers' use, but currently the room is ornamented by important pieces. The grand *dessert* or ornament for the banquet table is noteworthy. It is of Fernando VII's time, performed in the Porcelain Royal Factory of La Moncloa, that was the successor of the Buen Retiro Factory, where there also was an important workshop of hard stones.

At both sides of the fireplace, four out of the eight console tables of mahogany and gilded bronze, performed in 1791 according to a design of Francisco Sabatini for the Dining Room or Carlos IV's Antechamber, at this very same Palace. Atop, French clocks and two models of bronze and hard stones, proceeding from the Four River Fountain that Bernini performed at the Piazza Navona in Rome. The pictures above are two fine old copies of figures painted by Raphael in the *Stanza della Segnatura* of the Vatican Palace, and two *landscapes with mythological scenes* by B.M. Agüero, dating back to the end of the XVIIth century.

At the courtyard side there are two other console tables of the end of the XIXth century of carved and gilded wood, but their table tops are of marble and painted plaster, Italian from the XVIIth century; above them, a beautiful *round small temple with columns*, of the end of the XVIIIth century, from the Buen Retiro, and another one of bronze of the Trajan's column.

Both pictures, *Passages of Solomon's life*, by Luca Giordiano, served, along with others of the same subject and same artist, as models for the tapestries of the King's Room in this New Palace, woven at the Tapestry Royal Factory under Corrado Giaquinto's management. Of this same manufacture are the cloth ornamented with the royal coat of arms above the fireplace and the bench covers for the Chapel, all from the XVIIIth century.

Columns Hall

This Hall is the stairwell that according to Sacchetti's designs was supposed to serve to enter to the Queen's Room. Its walls are similar to

The Lavatory of the Maundy Thursday of 1875, 27 of March: Alfonso XII's first one. "Some time elapsed before the crowd issued from the chapel where the religious service was performed [...] We made thus our entrance into the hall of the columns which we found already crowded with spectators, more than 800 of whom were ladies, standing all round, somewhat cramped up on benches, row upon row, leaving barely the most limited space open for the performers. Within this space the twelve paupers, or apostles, sat on a settee, each of them with his best foot foremost -the foot and leg bare to the knee, and as well "prepared" for the occasion as by dint of much soap and water could be contrived. Entered in procession, the King in his grand uniform, with a towel tied round his waist, apron wise, followed by Cardinal Moreno in his scarlet robes and skull cap, and behind and all round them a grand staff of grandees and marshals, an array of golden uniforms [...] The procession came to a halt on the narrow space before the seated twelve. The Cardinal stepped forward, attended by a grandee holding basin an ewer, and sprinkled a few drops of perfumed water over each of the bare feet in succession. The King came after, kneeling before each foot, rubbing it slightly with his towel, then stooping upon it as if he meant to kiss it -but he didn't. The ceremony did not last many minutes."
Antonio C.N. GALLENGA: *Iberian reminiscences. Fifteen years' travelling impressions of Spain and Portugal.* London, 1883.

Athlete with a disc. Cast in bronze of an old statue brought from Rome by Velázquez in 1651.

After the Lavatory, the Supper.
"The twelve men then got up; they were marshalled with great pomp round the hall, then seated in a row on one side of a long table [...] In the rear of the table, on a high and lofty platform, stood the Court. In the middle, the Infanta Isabella [...] and a multitude of State and Palace dignitaries. On the extrem right stood the diplomatic body [...] The King and his inmediate suite were the only waiters at the table. Innumerable dishes were handed in at the door, and passed from hand to hand to these exalted attendants, who, ranged in front of the table, laid them before the humble guests [...] The curious sight, however, was that of the poor Twelve Apostles. Alone, seated where all else were standing, there they were, all demure, bewildered, and, to say the truth, extremely bored [...] too shy to dare to look at, le alone touch, the exquisite viands which were thus thrust temptingly under their perplexed noses, and were as swiftly shisked off to make room for still daintier delicacies [...] The farce ... lasted about an hour, at the end of which the *fanfare* gave the signal of departure. The King and his suite marched off in stately order; the Princess and the Court followed, and the apostolic paupers were shown to the kitchen, where they were treated to a more substantial meal; and each of them was a happy man, with his basket of broken victuals for his family, and 100 reales in his pocket."
Antonio C.N. GALLENGA: *Iberian reminiscences. Fifteen years' travelling impressions of Spain and Portugal,* London, 1883.

hose of the staircase that Sabatini carried out eventually. The ceiling is different since it was decorated already in Carlos III's day, who had disposed here the main staircase the way it is today, at the opposite side, and the stuccoes were already designed by Sabatini, and performed by Bernardino Rusca in 1761, simultaneously with the ones of the Halberdiers Hall; the four medaillons in bas-relief depict the four elements. Between 1762 and beginning of 1763 Giaquinto painted the fresco, the effect of which is, therefore, thought up to be perceived from the first flight of Sabatini's staircase. It is advisable to

Columns Hall: Tapestry with *The acts of the Apostles* according to Rafael Urbino's designs. Detail.

Neptune. Jonghellinck

watch it from a very close spot to the Room entrance and, if possible, squatted down. The subject implies an allusion to the King in the shape of Apollo as a sun deity, since it represents *The Sun before which appearance all the Nature forces rejoice and brighten up.* Apollo, who advances on his cart along the Zodiac ring, is accompanied by the Hours and preceded by the Dawn and the Zephyr. Lower down, the seasons of the year and the elements are symbolized by Ceres, Bacchus, Venus, Vulcan, Diana, Pan and Galatea.

View of the decoration in fresco of the vault of the Throne Hall: Apotheosis of the Spanish Monarchy. Giambattista Tiépolo.

The ceremonial order of the halls in the Palace was governed by the etiquette: each room was meant to a specific task and the access was progressively more restricted. The embryo of this kind of distribution, that goes back to the beginning of the XVIth century, is a two pieces core: the *room*, to receive, and the *chamber*, to sleep. By introducing other previous and intermediate ones arises the sequence of the King's Room: Waiting Room - Room - Anteroom - Antechamber - Chamber - small rooms or private sitting rooms. The same order prevailed in the rooms of the other royal persons, but with a decreasing amplitude predicated on the rank of each one.
"I was several times at court, during its residence here: all the royal family dine publicly in separate rooms; and it is the *etiquette* to visit each apartment whilst they are at dinner; a most tiresome employ for those who are obliged to be there, and it would be thought particular, if the foreign ambassadors were not constantly to attend: Don Luis, the King's brother, who is the lowest in rank is first visited ... the next in turn, is the Infanta Doña Maria [Josefa], who seemed to be a very inoffensive little woman. Then to the two Infantes, Don Gabriel y Don Antonio... Thence to the prince and princess of Asturias, the latter is of the house of Parma, and seems to be very affable".
William DALRYMPLE: *Travels through Spain and Portugal in 1774...*, London, 1777.

Also by Giaquinto, and his last work at the Palace, is *The Majesty of the Crown of Spain*, located right above the door. At the time it was painted this space was the staircase, and that image warned the visitors they were entering into the royal rooms.

Since Carlos V moved the ball room over here, this became the setting of the court banquets and parties that were not just for fun, but also for ceremonies. For instance, on Maundy Thursday the King washed feet and served supper to twelve poor people who symbolized the Apostles, before the court that attended the scene. **The Lavatory**, a pious habit that other European monarchs besides the Spanish one used to perform - and the Pope still does currently - kept on to be carried out till Alfonso XIII's reign. Precisely the tapestries that cover the arches illustrate *The Acts of the Apostles*, and they were woven in Brussels at the beginning of the XVIIth century following the cartoons that Raphael painted for the famous tapestry that is at the Vatican. Three of the bronze sculptures are also Flemish, a part of the series of the *Seven Planets* cast by Jonghellink around 1570: *Mars, Venus* and *Earth*. The fourth sculpture is a bronze copy of the *Gladiator with a disk*, commissioned by Velázquez in 1651 at Rome. The busts of emperors of porphyry and marbles are also Italian and from different epochs.

The large sculpture of *The Emperor Carlos V dominating the Fury* is a nineteenth-century copy commissioned to the Parisian

Throne Hall. Detail of the western end, with the paintings in fresco by G.B. Tiépolo and the stucco sculptures by Roberto Michel.

"However, to our great satisfaction, we gain admission to the whole of the State apartments, and their exceeding beauty and richness of decorations, together with the costly display of rare ornaments and furnitre, amply gratify our curiosity and desire."
John Benjamin STONE: *A tour with Cook through Spain... as seen and enjoyed in a summer holiday.* London, 1873.

bronzesmith Barbedienne, in 1878, of Leone Leoni's original that is situated at the Prado Museum. Its placing here in 1879, on a Neoplateresque pedestal, is a feature that evokes the glories of the Spanish branch of the Hapsburgs, linking them with those of the Bourbons, and it has to be understood in that sense within the reorganization of the spaces and the decoration of the Palace by Alfonso XII, who also carried out a room specifically planned for balls and gala lunches; thus, this Columns Hall was since then destined only to the more formal events, either of ritual like the Lavatory, or mournful, like the exposure of Queen Mercedes' corpse; or political, like the signing of the Treaty of the Adherence of Spain to the European Community in 1985.

The bronze chandeliers, also Parisian of about 1846, correspond, nevertheless, to the period when this Hall was most frequently utilized for parties and balls: i.e. during Queen Isabel II's reign.

From here it led to the anteroom (Carlos III's Antechamber) according to the ceremonial route in force since Carlos IV, but nowadays it follows, as far as possible, the order of the King's Room, under Carlos III, and therefore the entrance is through a secondary door, to the Throne Hall.

The Throne Hall
The Throne Hall (also called the Levee of the Royal Room, of Kingdoms, or of Ambassadors) keeps the entire ornamental

Throne Hall. Detail of the embroidery and of the golden carving, performed in Naples according G. Battista Natali's designs.

*Throne Hall. Detail of the frescoes.
Giambattista Tiépolo.*

Audience on the 8th of December 1783, festivity of the Immaculate, patron of Carlos III Order; the King returns from the ceremony at the Chapel.
"We got the Ambassadors Hall being almost the first ones. The pages were grouped around the brazier; they were dressed in blue and wore orange red stockings...Little by little a real crowd arrived and occupied the whole room. It could be stated that it is impossible to gather such a strange collection of personages, even looking for them here and there. My attention was struck by some Staff officers with their canes, many knights of any kind, and two Capuchins. Regarding the Hall, it is majestically upholstered with crimson velvet, with gold ornaments and embroidery of a great bulk. On the vault show some very beautiful figures, with typical Spanish features. The mirrors are of an extraordinary height and width. On cages there were parrots and other birds with plumage of the prettiest colors. The King, the crown Prince and the two Princes went trough the Hall in solemn gathering, coming from the Chapel. They wore large white cloaks with blue ornaments (of Carlos III Order), like the grandees and the high ranking court people who preceded and followed them".
Daniel Gotthilf MOLDENHAWER: *Account of the trip to Spain in 1782-1783, published by Emile Gigas*, Paris, 1927.

assemblage such as it was thought out and performed during Carlos III's reign, since it was totally finished in 1772. A recent restoration has returned all its splendor to this magnificent hall, by means of cleaning the fresco and changing the original velvet for a new one, moving the embroidery to the latter.

The Sovereign used to receive here all the ceremony audiences, up to the very last one, inasmuch as it was in this Hall where, according to the ceremonial, the King's dead body was displayed prior to its removal to the Pantheon of San Lorenzo el Real: the tables, the ornaments of the mirrors and the canopy were then taken away, and the hanging was changed.

Although Sacchetti had planned to cover all the walls of this gallery with marbles in order to frame the mirrors and bas-reliefs, nothing was done before Carlos III's arrival. The King decided that the decoration of this room be directed by his right-hand man in good taste matters, Count Gazzola, who commissioned the designs for the furniture to the architect from Piacenza Giovanni Battista Natali. Apparently the choice of the painter and of the sculptor who decorated the vault can also be attributed to Gazzola.

The magnificent effect of this union between painting, sculpture and decorative design reaches its highest point in the vault walls and

The Throne Hall

The Throne Hall.
"The largest and most magnificent hall of the Palace due to the superb mirrors and the rich furniture with which it is ornamented...Tiépolo was very imaginative and he painted as warmly as easily..."
Jean-François PEYRON: *Nouveau voyage en Espagne fait en 1777 et 1778, & Essais sur l'Espagne.*

Throne Hall. Prudence, ascribed to Foggini.

in the pelmets. The Chamber sculptor Roberto Michel, performed the ornamental stuccoes of the pelmets and the cornice, with a bright and fresh inventiveness comparable to those that the great Tiépolo showed in the vault, his last masterpiece, that has always been object of deserved praises among his own contemporaries.

Throne Hall. Detail of the frescoes, across the canopied Throne: Olympic Gods and personifications of the American provinces of the Spanish Crown, *Giambattista Tiépolo.*

"I had before seen all the palaces of the kings of England, France, Sardinia, Naples, Prussia, and Portugal; those of the pope, the emperor, and of several German princes; and I give the preference to this; but it may possibly be equalled by the palace which the king of Naples is now building at Caserta, and of which I saw part in 1769". Richard TWISS: *Travels through Portugal and Spain in 1772 and 1773.* London 1775.

Mars. *Jonghellinck.*

The grandeur and power of the Spanish Monarchy is here expressed through a large number of allegorical and allusive figures that expand on a background of open skies. When Tiépolo painted the fresco the access to the Hall was from the current Official Royal Antechamber, that used to be also an antechamber of the King's Room - and where the vault was also painted by him, with a similar subject - so that the composition has to be understood coming in from that side; advancing from there to about the half of the Hall the central group can be easily descried, that it is the *Spanish Monarchy* which throne, set on a large globe, is bordered by the statues of Apollo and Minerva, surrounded by the Science of Government, Peace and Justice - near of which the Virtue is flying - and by Abundance and Mercy. A ring of clouds surrounded by geniuses, one of whom holds the Royal Crown in the very center of the vault, serves as a canopy for the Monarchy throne. Behind all this section of the composition, and very appropriately placed, adjacent to the King's Room, is a pyramid or monument in Carlos III's honour, with the figures of the Magnanimity, the Glory, the Affability and the Advice, and very close those of the three theological virtues, plus the Prudence, the Fortitude and the Victory; finally, the Fine Arts "depicted in one of the vault angles, express with their attributes that are going to perpetuate the glories of the great prince who has been their restorer".

Such a glorification of the Monarchy and of the Sovereign constitutes the main part of the allegory: the other half of heaven that the vault pretends to be, the farthest from the access door, it is inhabited by the Olympus gods. Among them stand out Mercury, who, as the ambassador

Throne Hall. An angle with the furniture made in Naples according to G. Battista Natale's design.

The Public Audience.
"Coming into the Parade Square, the vehicle of the Papal Nuncio or Ambassador will pass through the parade or guard ranks, which, previously formed up, will do the ordinance honors, playing the Royal March...The Nuncio or Ambassador will alight at the foot of the staircase (*as only the royal people do*). The other individuals...will do it at the lateral doors of the Royal Palace, but inside. At the main staircase the Royal Halberdiers Guards companies with their band ahead, that will make the corresponding honors; also... the Major of the palace on weekly service and the so-called Gentlemen of "house and mouth" ...the head of the Foreign Affairs Department Protocol escorts him to the Audience Hall, where he is received by the Sovereign, seated on the throne, having, at his right-hand side, the Princes, and at his left-hand side, the Ministries and the high dignitaries of the Palace: at both sides of the Hall are standing the foreign Ministries and Courtiers. The Ambassador, accompanied by his Secretaries and attachés, approaches to the throne, and salutes three times; the Prince takes off his hat in the way of salute, and points him out the armchair that he has to occupy before the throne: the Ambassador sits down, and putting on his hat, makes a solemn speech...Whereupon the Sovereign answers him, and thus, the audience finishes".
Palatial Guide, nr. 19, Madrid, 1899.

of the gods before the Monarchy, seems to announce the Peace on behalf of Jupiter; Apollo, sun god and Arts protector, is exactly over the King's throne; at the left hand-side of the latter stands Mars throwing out the Crime and the Furies and, opposite the throne, in a dominating place, Neptune.

The canopied Throne, in the Throne Hall. In the Fernando VII style carpet: Both Worlds, an Eighteenish emblem of the territorial area of the old Spanish Monarchy.

Royal Audience or "Levee"

"For ceremonials, no doubt, here must be place. The most regular among these is the irksome farce of dining under public inspection. That of *besamanos,* or the payment of respect, is only permitted on festival-days. It is performed in Indian file, to borrow a military idea, and with Indian rapidity. Still it lasts long enough to exercise, and indeed exhaust, the patience of some of the brances of the royal family, who do not seem to be duly possessed of that very necessary quality of their high rank. In this ceremonious procedure, which takes place before the royal family (not party, for each individual has his dining apartment), sits down to table, the file of personages who present themselves, diplomatists, military and official people, all in short of due rank to place themselves in file and full dress, meander through te place, from one apartment to another, each person, on his knee, kissing the hand of the royal personage into whose presence he comes; the business or ceremonial concluding with the termination of the file." Maurice KEATING: *Travels through France and Spain to Morocco* (1785). London, 1817.

Down at the lowest part of the fresco, on top of the cornice, extends a numerous range of characters, who perhaps are the most excelling part of this composition. They represent the kingdoms of the Iberian Peninsula and the countries then under the Crown of Spain: at the entrance side, Andalusia, Catalonia, Aragon, Castile and Granada; at the opposite side, the East Indies, besides the Basque Country, Cantabria, Asturias and Murcia; and at the long side over the balconies, starting from the most remote end, America, with Christopher Columbus and several figures alluding to the Discovery, and thereafter León, Galicia, Valencia and

Throne Hall.
Ornamental top of a mirror.

"The state-apartments are large, well proportioned, and handsomely decorated: but it contains no vast gallery, and no instance of superior magnificence ... indeed the grandeur of this palace entirely consist in the continued suite of handsome and well-furnished apartments."
George Downing WHITTINGTON: *Travels through Spain and part of Portugal.* London, 1808.

Extremadura. It is not easy to identify them since Tiépolo has created them with the great freedom of an artist, in a fantastic exotic key and not concerned at all for rigor, but with grace and picturesque dash both in its entirety and in the details, such as that page who, just above the throne, is trying to catch a macaw, right in front of the group that alludes America.

The rest of the decoration, including the console tables, the mirrors, the canopy, the armchair and the hanging, should be understood as a whole conceived by Gazzola and the Italian artists that he had chosen, bringing everything from there all elements, what indicates Carlos III's adherence to the Naples formulae.

The velvet was woven *expressly* at Genoa, thereby obtaining an exceptional quality, and later on it was sent to Naples to be embroidered by the needleman of that Court, Andrea Cotardi, or Gottard, with a gilded silver thread. Among the various designs that were requested from Madrid, Paris and Naples were chosen those submitted by Giovanni Battista Natale, an innate from Piacenza, as was Gazzola, and who likewise did the design of the console tables and of the mirrors performed by the carver Gennaro di Fiore. Between the summer of 1765 and November of the following year all the decorative elements for the Royal Audience or "levee" hall became ready, although they did not occupy the place for which they were conceived until 1772.

The ornamental group designed by Natale is a key work of the Italian rococo fantasy. With Tiépolo's magnificent exoticness, vaguely alluding to the wide dominium of the Spanish Monarchy, perfectly

Throne Hall. Bronze lions.
Matteo Bonicelli, 1651.

"The Muses". *Detail of the fresco at Carlos III's Anteroom:* Trajan's Apotheosis. *Antonio Rafael Mengs.*

"The room where the throne is, and the one called *Hall of the Kingdoms*, are worthy of admiration even after visiting the Gallery of Versailles. A Venetian called Tiépolo has painted in fresco on its vault the different garments of the vast Spanish Monarchy, a kind of decoration that only can correspond to the Palace of the Sovereign of Spain...The mirrors, of a size probably unique in Europe, have been manufactured in San Ildefonso...".
Jean-François BOURGOING: *Nouveau voyage en Espagne...*Paris, 1788.

"The chief saloon, or Hall of Ambassadors, is by far the richest and grandest room in the palace; indeed, I cannot help thinking it is the most magnificent chamber in Europe [...] The throne is the perfection of grandeur..."
John Benjamin STONE: *A tour with Cook through Spain...as seen and enjoyed in a summer holiday.* London, 1873.

agree the characteristic subjects of the late baroque that Natale has arranged in the decorative carving of the twelve mirrors and matching tables: the four parts of the world, the four seasons of the year - or the four epochs of life - and four virtues; the whole shapes thus a nice rhetorical praise of the power that has there its seat.

The bronze sculptures adorning the Hall were also placed then, but all are of a prior date: the four cardinal virtues that are at the Throne wall are ascribed to René Fremin, as performed for the altarpiece of the La Granja Collegiate Church, nevertheless they have been also attributed to Foggini. *Mercury, Jupiter, Saturn* and *Mars* form, along with the other three that are in the Columns Hall, the *Seven Planets* series due to Jonghellinck; the other two, a *Satyr* and the *Germanic*, are molded from classical statues commissioned by Velázquez and carried out at Rome. The bronze lions are also Roman and of 1651, by Mateo Bonicelli, that the distinguished painter commissioned to decorate the Mirror Hall at the Alcazar.

The two rock crystal and silver chandeliers were acquired in 1780 to the Venice ambassador, Francesco Pesaro, under Sabatini's warm recommendation. It is paradoxical that such pieces of furniture completed this rococo group when their style already was outdated, and just ten years before Sabatini began to plan for this Hall, at Carlos IV's request, a new decoration, radically architectonic and classicist of marbles and bronzes, with Corinthian pilasters that was never ended.

Carlos IV must be credited with to the acquisition of three out of the four splendid clocks having a complex hour and musical mechanism: at

KING CARLOS III'S ROOM

Carlos III's Anteroom.

"Fame proclaiming Trajan's name".
Detail of the fresco: Trajan's
Apotheosis, *Antonio Rafael Mengs*.

the right-hand side of the canopy, a big grandfather clock with an ebony and bronzes box Louis XVI style, performed by Fernando Berthoud, in Paris around 1780; at the left side, another one also of ebony and bronzes of rococo style, English, by John Ellicot. Opposite, a monumental table clock by Furet and Godon of white marble and bronze, representing the Music and the Astronomy; and of the same materials and taste -Louis XVI, around 1780-, on the closest console table, another by "Godon, clockmaker and machinist of SMC". Fernando VII respected the decoration of his grandfather's time, but adding the large carpet woven at the Royal Factory of Madrid. To his reign and to his father's reign correspond the Empire style candelabra on the console tables.

Finally, that what grants the Hall's name: the *Throne*. The original armchair, of which the two that stay here are an accurate copy, is located at the La Granja Palace having Carlos III's portrait in the relief that tops the back. Alfonso XII ordered to copy this furniture, placing his profile on the medallion; Alfonso XIII followed suit, adding another one with Queen Victoria Eugenia's portrait in order to place both

The King's lunch.

"His Majesty has lunch by himself in the Room reserved for this purpose, and it is there, seated at the table, where the Ministries pay their respects to him. As soon as the King begins to eat his lunch, they greeted him and thereafter would proceed on their way to the Prince's Room, who was also having his lunch. Later on they came back to the King, a little before the table was cleared. Sometimes they would accompany him to his private sitting room and stay there with him about a quarter of an hour; that is when the King uses to chat with some of them. A gentleman puts the dishes on the King's table as soon as they are passed to him; later on the pages carry them away. The one who presents water or wine to the King gets on his knees when he starts drinking. During the whole meal the Nuncio remains standing a few steps before the table, and the King talks almost exclusively to him. Once the King is through eating, the Patriarch, who is a prelate and, therefore, is dressed like the Nuncio and the Confessor, says the thanksgiving prayer that takes hardly two or three seconds. The King makes the sign of the Cross, cleans his mouth and his hands and goes into his Room.

...I also saw the Prince during his lunch. He eats only with the Princess, who is waited on by two ladies. As the Prince does, she was talking from time to time to one or another ambassador.

...Right after the lunch was over, the King changed his clothes and went hunting".

Daniel Gotthilf MOLDENHAWER: *Story of his travel to Spain in 1782-1783, published by Emile Gigas. Paris, 1927.*

together; likewise, the current ones show the images of Their Majesties don Juan Carlos and doña Sofia.

Carlos III's Anteroom

The Anteroom was the room where the King used to have his meals and to grant the ordinary audiences. At that time, its walls were covered during the winter with the tapestries of David, Solomon and Absalon History series, woven at the Royal Factory of Tapestries while during the summer they were with eight large equestrian portraits, main works of Rubens and Velázquez, nowadays at the Prado Museum. But from Fernando VII's reign on the pictures that are there include four by Jordan, two about *Solomon's Life*, and the remaining two pertain to the Roman history: *Qunto Curcio jumping into the chasm* and *Seneca's death*.

In the vault stands out the painting on fresco of A.R. Mengs, *Apotheosis of Trajan*, of 1774. This Roman emperor born in Hispania, used here as Carlos III's "alter ego", is shown at the side of the vault opposite to the entrance sitting on his throne, wearing the imperial purple and surrounded by Minerva, Hercules and the Glory that is crowning him. Diverse allegories of the Victory and of her virtues are grouped at the long sides, while at the opposite wall the nine Muses and the Arts, among other personifications, encircle the Apollo temple. It is quite a discourse about the illustrated Monarch's virtues, his protection to Arts, etc.

The stucco designed by Sabatini was performed by Andrioli between 1761 and 1763. Also of Carlos III's reign are all the marble elements and the four console tables and their corresponding mirrors although at that time they were not yet here. From Paris, as did the two large "Fernando VII" style chandeliers, proceeded the circular couch, with Thomire's bronzes and Isabel II's initials in the upholstery; it dates from 1846, but it was not placed here until the end of the XIXth century, when the long coaches were placed along the walls; the stools are of the same period. The carpet, of the Royal Factory, is dated in 1880; to these years belongs the silk of the wall, that due to its bad condition has been copied and replaced in 1994.

Since Carlos IV ordered to place the main staircase at its current location, this Anteroom, which directly led to the Hall of Columns, was the first compartment of the King's Room, that from here on continued towards the Orient, in an inversive order than Carlos III's one, assigned by then to the Prince of Asturias.

Carlos III's Antechamber.

The Antechamber or "Room of the Conversation" was where the King had supper, and likewise it is represented -although "making up" the vault- in Paret's picture *Carlos III having dinner before his court*. The tapestries that then decorated it were those of Joseph's Story, performed

Carlos III's Antechamber.

at the Royal Factory on cartoons painted in 1770 by José del Castillo, under Giaquinto's management, but during the summer they used to hang here Titian's, Van Dyck's and Velázquez's masterpieces, such as the Meninas. To this room were assigned the magnificent console tables of hard stones and bronzes, a masterpiece of the Buen Retiro Royal Factory, and that nowadays are at the Prado Museum.

From Carlos III's reign the marble decoration still subsists, and also from then dates the fireplace, very good and that -unusually- still keeps its bronzes. But the painting, both of the vault and of the pictures, is the absolute protagonist of this Room.

The fresco by Antonio Rafael Mengs depicts *The Apotheosis of Hercules:* the hero, traditionally utilized in Spain as the King's personification or emblem, is welcome by the gods in the Olympus

Carlos IV. *Francisco de Goya.*

The King's dinner.
"At dinner, pages bring in the different dishes, and presenting them to one of the lords in waiting, he places them upon the table; another nobleman stands on the King's side, to hand him his wine and water, which he tastes, and presents on his knee; the primate is there to say grace; the inquisitor-general also attends at a distance, on one side, and the captain, who has the guard, on the other; the ambassadors are in a circle near him, with whom he converses for a short time, when they retire into a room behind his chair; the rest of the court form in a second circle, without the ambassadors, at the end of the room; when he rises from table, all who are to be introduced to him are presented; and the governor of Madrid, having received the parole, he enters the room to the ambassadors: he goes out a sporting every day of the year, rain or blow, whilst at Madrid, once a day, in the afternoon; but in the country, at the *Sitios,* morning and evening."
William DALRYMPLE: *Travels through Spain and Portugal in 1774...,* London, 1777.

as a reward to his great feats: the purpose is to praise Carlos III as an eminent military man and an expert in politics, as well as a patron of the Arts, to which alludes the beautiful group of Apollo and the Muses above the entrance door. The restraint decorative stuccoes, carried out by Bernardino Rusca, were designed as well

Maria Luisa of Parma, dressed as a"maja". *Francisco de Goya.*

"Mars and other olympic gods"
Detail from the frescoes of the vault of Carlos III's Antechamber, The Apotheosis of Hercules, Antonio Rafael Mengs.

by the painter and not by Sabatini. The latter yielded to his friend Mengs after confronting Giaquinto, who initially was supposed to decorate this vault. The incident with his two rivals, favored by the King, decided Fernando VII's painter to leave Spain, already old and tired. The four oval reliefs at the corners are by Felipe de Castro.

Apollo, Bacchus and other olympic gods. *Detail from the frescoes of the vault of Carlos III Antechamber,* The Apotheosis of Hercules, *by Antonio Rafael Mengs.*

"The apartments are (or rather were before the queen-mother took toll) gorgeous in the extreme, in their fittings-up, etc. The number of state rooms is almost interminable; and all have their ceilings beautifully painted. The majority of the finest removable pictures once adorning the walls are, however, now at the Museo. I can give you no further account of the interior, in consequence of its being in the actual occupation of the young Queen."
ANONYMOUS: *Spain, Tangier, etc., visited in 1840 and 1841. By X.Y.Z.* London, 1845

The pictures, masterpieces of Goya, are two couples of portraits of *Carlos IV* and of his wife Queen *Maria Luisa of Parma*: one is more formal, showing the King wearing a uniform of Royal Guard colonel and the Queen dressed in a Court cloth; while the other one, more casual, he is wearing a hunting attire while she is dressed à la Spanish "maja", with an outer skirt and a mantilla. These are the most outstanding canvases that can be contemplated at the Palace, and the two first mentioned have been in this Room since Fernando VII's reign. The contrast with Goya's work constitute the busts of the same royal couple, in marble, by J. Adán (1797).

Also from Carlos IV's reign are the console tables and the monumental mahogany and bronze clock in the shape of a small temple, with a flute organ -housed at the base- and the alabaster sculptures: the main one represents *Cronos holding the celestial sphere*. The design is attributed to J.D. Dugourc. It is the last work (1799) of the clockmaker Louis Godon, a distinguished purveyor of Parisian decorative objects for Carlos IV.

Carlos III's Chamber, called of Gasparini.

The Chamber was the place where the King would dress and receive the private audiences. Therefore we should not be surprised about the delicacy with which Carlos III willed to decorate it, entrusting the design, for all and each element, to his royal painter Matías Gasparini, whom he had come along with him from Naples: it is logical that the artist's name serve to name this Room of the Palace since Fernando VII's day, inasmuch as the marble floor, the stucco vault, the hanging embroidered in silk with gold and silver threads, the furniture of precious woods and bronzes, everything

The ceremony of "covering" a Grandee of Spain.

"It is held in the Antechamber, as all the events of a great etiquette... while the Grandees who must be covered are waiting their turn, accompanied by their godfathers, in the Anteroom, the invited Ladies and the covered Grandees are waiting in the Antechamber, the screen that gives access to the Chamber opens up, appears Her Majesty followed by her high staff of servants and, after an elaborated court reverence, sits down... and addressing to the Ladies who are at her right-hand side, she states: *have a seat*, and to the Grandees, who are at her left-hand side: *put your hats on*...The appointee gets into the regal room, who is led, by his godfather's right hand, while the Major of the Palace on duty is leading him by his left hand. The Ladies stand up when he comes in and the Grandees take off their hats; the neophyte and his companions, two steps away from the door, bow for the first time before Her Majesty, at the center of the hall they bow for the second time, and finally for the third time once they are near the Royal Person. Upon withdrawing of the godfather and the major of the palace, the Queen says: *put your hat on and talk*...(at this point there were nuances predicated on the rank of nobility) thereafter he takes off his hat and kneeling, he kisses the Royal hand...".
Palatial Guide, nr. 31, Madrid, 1900.

Carlos III's Chamber, or Gasparini Hall. Detail

Carlos III's Chamber. Detail of the embroidered hanging.
Mattia Gasparini and his crew, detail.

was designed by Gasparini, who until his death directed this top work of the *barochetto*, that was continued under the supervision of his widow and son and of his successor at the post of "chamber decorator", G.B. Ferroni.

Performed by Italian artificers and German cabinetmakers, this room can claim to be from Madrid only because it was commissioned

Carlos III's Chamber. Detail of set of chairs of fine woods, bronzes and embroidered tapestry according to Mattia Gasparini's designs, detail.

Maria Luisa of Parma, dressed in Court clothes. *Francisco de Goya.*

in said city by one who had been king of Naples, and as a matter of fact it is an international work and one of the most perfect of the European late baroque. The vegetal and asymmetrical ornamentation of the rococo shines on its maximum splendor, full of an exotic fantasy of a Chinese inspiration. One cannot help to admire its magnificence, but to find its taste and to joyfully get lost among its extremely rich arabesques it is necessary to forget about Goya and Mengs, escaping to the dream world that the Throne Hall also suggests.

This ornamental has remained entirely untouched, and definitely more complete than when its artificer and the Monarch who commissioned it were able to contemplate it, since the performance of so much work took a long time: as the embroidered hanging was not finished until 1802, fourteen years after Carlos III's death, during that reign the walls were covered in wintertime with Royal Factory tapestries - on Antonio Gónzalez Velázquez's cartoons, according to David Teniers' style, of whom the King was so fond -, and in summertime with works of Diego Velázquez, such as *Vulcan's Forge, The Tapestry Weavers* and *The Drinkers*, besides "Murillo's", "Ribera's" and "Titian's". Since the King admired Mengs very much the latter work of that painter was placed here, *The Annunciation*, currently at the Royal Chapel.

To Gasparini is also due the design of the box of the small English clock - of Martineau - that stands on the console table between the balconies. Much more important, both for its beautiful style Louis XV box and for its complex machinery with music and automatons, is the shepherd's clock, built by Jacques Droz at Switzerland and acquired by Fernando VI in 1756.

Carlos III's chamber or Gasparini Hall.

Chinese stuccoes. Gennaro de Matteis and others, according to Mattia Gasparini's designs.

Detail of a frieze coming from Carlos III's "private sitting rooms of woods from the Indies".

The embroidered hanging was not placed until 1815. Alfonso XII ordered to restore it, and since then the curtains, also embroidered, that used to cover doors and windows are stored away. In the last great campaign of restoration the embroidery has been moved to a new silk background.

Except for the superb set of chairs of chosen woods and bronzes, no element of the furniture corresponds to Gasparini's group. From Carlos IV's day are the first class console tables, with Domingo Urquiza's bronzes and cabinetmaking from the royal workshop, and the French candelabra, among which are outstanding those of "Etruscan" taste of porcelain and bronze. The superb chandelier is the one with a greater symbolic meaning among the multifarious commissioned by Fernando VII, showing his monogram and that of his third wife Maria Josefa Amalia of Saxony. The table already corresponds to the Isabelline period. It was designed and performed at Rome by Gerardo Volponi and Guglielmo Chidel, under Filippo Agricola's direction in 1848.

Three adjoining small rooms that are not open to public were Carlos III's offices, called "rooms of Indies woods", due to the rich decoration, also managed by Gasparini, and which later on was dismantled and installed in other rooms of the Palace. Fernando VII, who also used them for his study or *small room*, had Luis López paint their vaults on fresco.

Carlos III's "Tranvía"

This room had its current layout in 1880, when the passage between Gasparini and the new Gala Dining Room was meant to free; from

Carlos III's Chamber or Gasparini Hall. Detail of the Chinese stuccoes, at the vault, and of the embroidered hanging.

A free visitor.
"Not a door being closed, I penetrated through the chamber of the throne even into the old king's sleeping-apartment [Charles III]... In this room, as in all the others I passed through, without any exception, stood cages of gilded wire, of different forms and sizes, and in every cage a curious exotic bird, in full song, each trying to out-sing his neighbour. Mingled with hese warblings was heard at certain intervals the low chime of musical clocks, stealing upon the ear like the tones of harmonic glasses. No other sound broke in any degree the general stillness, except, indeed, the almost inaudible footsteps of several aged domestics, in court-dresses of the cut and fashion prevalent in the days of the king's mother, Elizabeth Farnese, gliding along quietly and cautiously to open the cages... I availed myself of the light reflected from a clear sun-set to examine the pictures, chiefly of a religious cast, with which these stately apartments are tapestried, particularly the Madonna del Spasimo... I stood fixed in the contemplation of this holy vision... till the approaching shadows of night had overspread every recess of these vast apartments... The song of the birds had ceased, as well as the soft diapason of the self-played organs; all was hushed, all tranquil."
William BECKFORD: *Italy; with sketches of Spain and Portugal...*(1787). London, 1834.

that time comes also its name (streetcar), that alludes to its narrow and long shape. Two rooms were here till then: one used only as a passageway, as nowadays, very small but literally covered by pictures in the reigns of Carlos III and Carlos IV, and overfilled with furniture in that of Isabel II; the other room, more interior and wider, was Carlos III Oratory, with access through the Chamber. It was designed by Sabatini, its walls were richly covered with Lanjarón marble and gilded bronzes worked in 1767-1768 by Urquiza, Vendetti and Beya: the vault with stuccoes, by Bernardino Rusca; the high altar was a Mengs's fresco, *The Adoration of the shepherds*. Other similar oratories, designed and built by Sabatini with an analogous richness, were also dismantled at the end of the XIXth century. These spaces destined to the morning and night devotion were important in the quotidian life of the royal people.

Currently there are here two console tables dating back to around 1780 which design is ascribed to Sabatini: two portraits, *Francisco of Portugal*, attributed to Ranc, and *Jacob (III) Stuart*, ascribed to Francisco Trevisani; and a cartoon for tapestry, *The wild boar hunting*, of José del Castillo. In the revamping campaign of 1991 new fabric covering the walls of this room was set and it was personalized with Don Juan Carlos' and Doña Sofía's monograms.

Carlos III's Room
This Room was meant for a bedroom already in the first plans for the royal rooms arrangement, and in fact it was so from Carlos III in 1764 to the 13th of December 1788, when he died here.

Detail of the Allegory of The Institution of the Carlos III Order, *Vicente López.*

"Peking", a Chinese fabric from the XVIIIth century with which the royal bedrooms and private sitting rooms were hung with tapestries in the summertime.

Nothing remains of the original furniture, that had been managed by Sabatini, and in which the tapestries, the carved and golden chairs by Chiani and Balce and the very rich fireplace bronzes of Vendetti did stand out. The paintings, about the Passion of Christ, were all by Mengs: four on top of the doors and a large *Descent* by Salvador Maella where *Carlos III*'s portrait is hanging at the present time in which the so called illustrated Monarch is dressed in the ceremony habit of the honourable Order that he had instituted to decorate the merit, and which order he had named after him, putting it under the patronage of the Immaculate Conception, to whom he had a very special devotion. In fact the current aspect of this Room is a kind of sanctuary dedicated to Carlos III, and to his Order, by his grandson Fernando VII, as the latin inscription at the vault reads: "To Carlos III, a deeply religious Monarch, instituting the Spanish Order under the Immaculate Virgin's protection / To reward the virtue and the merit / Under the same roof where he passed away and to receive a greater and heavenly recompense for his virtue and his merit / His grandson Fernando VII wanted that he be painted in the year 1828". Fernando VII, who had been using this Room also as bedroom when he was a Prince, turned it into his "dressing room" being a King.

The furniture of white and golden wood is typically "Fernandino" style; the elegant neoclassical new fireplace of Ionic order in white, rosy and green marble, seems to be Italian. The blue silk hanging with superposed white motifs allusive to the Order is also "Fernandino" style: stripes, stars, castles, lions and Carlos III's monograms; it is the

Carlos III's Hall

"In regard to its interior, is a world of wonders: everything that can ever exist insofar as the most rich and variegated in any kind of furniture, in magnificent hanging, in sumptuous draperies, decorate the rooms and the vast halls of stucco walls or brightly covered with delicate porcelain; the purple, the gold, the marble, the crystal seem to compete to reflect the light against a thousand different objects and make the splendid paintings stand out in which the best masters have known how to brighten up this gorgeous residence of the Kings of Spain with the most diverse topics taken from the Mythology, the Religion and the History getting to produce sometimes a full illusion".
A. MATHIEU: *L'Espagne, lettres d'un Français à un ami*. Madrid 1887.

Carlos III. *Mariano Salvador Maella.*

original hanging, except for the blue silk background that has been replaced twice, the first one during Alfonso XII's reign and the second at the 1986 restoration.

In addition to the overall effect, the most remarkable fact of this decorative campaign is the painting on fresco at the vault, where Vicente López represented *The Institution of the Carlos III Order*: the King, in full dress and with all the emblems proper of the sovereignty, is kneeling down before the Immaculate. Near the altar are the personifications of Religion, Pity, Gratitude, the Spanish Monarchy, the Public Happiness and Pleasure. On the southern wall, that is, above the fireplace, Honesty, Honor, Merit and Virtue are shown; and on the opposite one, an allegory of Peace benefits, accompanied by "the noble Agriculture" and several children throwing weapons to a blazing abyss, where also the dragon of Discord is joining in, while Evil and Rebellion Escape. Over the balconies, History, Time and Fame. The stucco decoration in the cornice, by José Tomás and José Ginés, completes that of the fresco: at the angles, held up by geniuses, there are four emblems allusive to the King; and in the central section three reliefs about the establishment of the Order and its aims.

Fernando VII kept Mengs' pictures in their original locations, and he ornamented this dressing room of his with furniture that no longer is here, since the console tables and the Fernandino mirrors were replaced under Alfonso XIII by the current ones, that are rococo style and therefore pertaining to an earlier time. Of the immense profusion of decorative bronze objects that were here two extraordinary pieces

Porcelain Private Sitting Room.

Detail of the Porcelain Private Sitting Room.

kept in their spots: the chandelier in the shape of a *fleur-de-lys*, the heraldic symbol of the Bourbon Dynasty, purchased in Paris about 1825 following Fernando VII's orders for this Room; and the amphora clock (towards 1800), of gilded and blued bronze, with a clock and automatons by J.F. De Belle, also from Paris.

Although it was not placed here until Isabel II's reign - who otherwise fully respected the "Fernandino" style decoration of this Room - the sumptuous *Pedestal table of Carlos X's crowning* (1825), of bronze and Sèvres porcelain, a present from the French Monarch to his Spanish counterpart, also dates back to Fernando VII's reign.

Porcelain Room
Influenced by his wife, who was a Saxon, Carlos III had created near Naples the famous Capodimonte Porcelain Factory, the workers

Yellow Room

The Art of painting.

"Emulation, it is to be supposed, has made them all do their best. In my private opinion *Corrado's* invention is more fanciful and various than that of the rest: but *Mengs* is by far the best painter, as his invention is not much inferior to *Corrado's,* his design much more correct, and his colouring quite magick. The King thinks him the greatest painter of the age; and as His Majesty has been from his infancy used to live in apartments rich ind pictures of the best kind, his opinion must certainly carry a great weight, whatever contempt some cyniks may affect for the connoisseurship of a king. Some other of those ceilings are to be ornamented with various carvings, gildings and stucco's, and some other still in other manners. But, as I said, every thing is at present in the utmost confusion, as nothing is perfectly finished... But besides the rich furniture destined to each of the royal apartments, some pieces of which are already placed, the King is possessed of an immense collection of Italian and Flemish pictures, part of which is intended for those apartments... It is to be hoped, when the palace is perfectly finished and furnished, that the King will order a catalogue and description of them, along with the plan and elevation of this magnificent fabrick, for the farther advancement of the polite arts, and the satisfaction of those who love them."

Joseph BARETTI: *Journey from London to Genoa, through England, Portugal, Spain and France* (in 1760). London, 1770.

and materials of which he had brought along with him to Madrid in 1760, setting up the Buen Retiro Royal Factory. He wanted to have at his Spanish palaces a porcelain room like the one of the Portici palace, and he commenced with the one in Aranjuez. Only when it was completed, from 1765 on, began the manufacturing of another "Porcelain Room" for the Madrid Palace, finishing its installation in 1771. The porcelain work is due to the same team, directed by José Gricci, but it has always been pointed out the drastic change of taste that can be noticed between both rooms: as opposed to the Chinese shapes and themes in Aranjuez, directly linked to the one in Portici designed by Natali, the room in Madrid adopts classicist late-baroque shapes that, in general, have been less appreciated than the open rococo of the other room. The design is near to Ferroni's taste, but the author is unknown. The names of the painters Juan Bautista de la Torre and Jenaro Boltri, employees of the Factory, have been cited in that regard. The splendid china and

Yellow Room: Sécretaire. *Forestier and Thomire, about 1790.*

Yellow Room. Tapestry drapes that adorned Carlos III's bedroom.

bronze vases come also from the Buen Retiro but of a very different taste from that of the walls, since they are already of Carlos IV's epoch, like the console tables on which they stand, of carved and painted wood.

Yellow Room

The name of this Room - and that of Crowns Room as it was called in the XIXth century - to the drapery that Fernando VII had placed; several tapestry cloths woven at the Royal Factory on José del Castillo's cartoons cover nowadays the walls, and under Francisco Sabatini's management, for Carlos III bedroom, and that besides covering the walls it included the curtains of doors and balconies, those of the bed and its bedspread, and the seats and other furniture pieces, as well as both sides of the fireplace screen, that here play the rôle of pelmets. The yellow silk framing the panels was revamped in 1995.

At the beginning of Carlos III's reign this Room was planned as the

Chandelier-Clock, *according to J.D. Dugourc's designs.*

Queen's Private Sitting Room, alluded by the topic of the fresco painted by Gian Doménico Tiépolo, *June in her chariot.* From 1766 on it was at Carlos III's service, who filled to bursting it with Teniers' and Brueghel's pictures, and excellent small portraits of Van Dyck and Velázquez. From that period still subsists the baseboard of fine woods marquetry carried out by German cabinetmakers of the workshop run by Gasparini.

Fernando VII had here his bedroom. He ordered to erase Tiépolo's fresco and that Luis López painted a new one, which topic is related to the new destiny of the room: June, on her golden chariot drawn by peacocks, accompanied by Hymen, is heading for the place where Dream sleeps.

The French furniture gathered here are the most outstanding of the Palace; they were designed by Jean-Demosthène Dugourc, an important decorator who worked a lot for Carlos IV, first at France and later on in Madrid, performing pieces of work that mark the transitional period between Louis XVI taste and the Empire style. The chest of drawers and the *secrétaire* carried out about 1790 by Forestier and Thomire still correspond to the first one. The rest of the furniture are characteristic pieces of the "Etruscan style", a genre of which Dugourc was a pioneer, and a forerunner of the Empire style. The very rich pedestal table, inspired in pieces of furniture found at Pompeii and Herculaneum, carries a horizontal clock performed by Godon with five circles indicating hours, months, calendar and weekly periods. The six armchairs also follow archaeological models not Spanish at all, in spite of the similarity of their backs with an ornamental comb; they belong to those carried out for queen Maria Luisa' s quarters at the Aranjuez Palace. Also from about 1800, but from Madrid, are the carpet from the Royal Factory, the two vases of the Buen Retiro and the clock on the bureau, signed by Manuel Gutiérrez. The lamp is "Fernandino" style - although not the one that was then here - as are the candelabra; the wall lamps, of Isabel II's reign, when the king consort don Francisco de Asis had here his dressing room. From Alfonso XII on it serves as sitting room and leads to the Gala Banquet Room.

QUEEN'S ROOM: THE BANQUET ROOM AND ADJACENT HALLS

Banquet Room

The large hall for dances and gala dinners strikes us for its length, since it is the result of having unified the three central rooms of the Western façade. These three rooms, and the other three interior corresponding ones that receive light from the main courtyard, formed during Carlos III's reign the Queen's Room, meant for that Monarch's spouse but who never did occupy it, since she died in 1760 before the Palace were in an inhabitable condition, but the queen mother Isabel of Farnese. The halls facing the galleries served as antechambers; the last

"The *Besamanos* is a terribly fussy and operose *función:* it is literally what it calls itself, and not only those who attend it, kiss hands, but every inmate of the palace, down to the porters and scullions..."
Mrs. William PITT BYRNE: *Things of Spain and the Spaniards as they are.* London, 1866.

one led to the *room for meals and levees*, that corresponds to the most remote section from the access door; the central area was the *chamber*, and the closest to the King's quarters was the *bedroom*, an arrangement logically thought in order that the rooms of the regal spouses were most intimately linked.

Occupied later on by the Princess Maria Josefa and by the Princess of Asturias, this room was used again by the Queen during Fernando VII's reign, who ordered to carry out important revamping and decoration works. Under Isabel II's reign it was occupied by the king consort don Francisco de Asís, but when, after the First Republic, the Restoration of the Monarchy returned the Throne to the Bourbons, Alfonso XII desired to have at the Palace, in lieu of so many living quarters with large and medium size halls and small studies, a large salon where gala banquets for more than one hundred people could be served. Therefore he commissioned in 1879 to his architect José Segundo de Lema to unify these three halls propping up the transversal walls on basket-handle arches, so that both the structure and the decoration of the vaults would remain intact. The works did not finish until 1885.

Banquet Room

French fruit-bowl. XIXth century. Fernando VII's glassware.

Fresco of the central vault of the Banquet Room, Columbus offering the New World to the Catholic Monarchs, *Antonio Gónzalez Velázquez.*

The architect succeeded in giving coherence to a space clearly sectioned in three parts and where the ceiling decoration is Eighteenish, while on the walls the influence of the contemporaneous French neo-baroque taste is obvious not only in the design, in which are amalgamated details of various origins mainly Louis XVI, but in the materials, since the columns are of Bagnéres marble and the great majority of the bronze work was carried out in Paris, including the fifteen chandeliers and the ten wall lamps. Also from Paris come the one hundred forty-four chairs for the fellow guests when they reach the maximum number; the table was never thought but as a frame without value as a furniture, collapsible in order to use the Room also for balls.

In regard to the wall decoration the choice made was a solution very much in line with the historicist taste of the epoch, covering the free spaces with tapestries from the Royal Collection, a part of the series called of *Vertummus and Pomona*, woven at the end of the XVIth century in Brussels by Pannemaker, on Vermeyer's cartoons. The "Alfonsina" decoration of the room is completed with twelve large *Chinese earthenware jars* of the XVIIIth century, and several large French

Fresco of the central vault of the Banquet Room, Boabdil handing the key of Granada to the Catholic Monarchs, Francisco Bayeu.

vases from the XIXth century, of golden bronze and porcelain of the Sévres manufacturing placed in the balcony recesses: six in a series of historic scenes related to the kings of France and Spain, painted by Lachassagne and Renaud (1830) and the other two, already of the mid-century, with landscapes, that are those placed in the first and in the last balcony.

To wrap it up let us watch the frescoes painted to decorate this Queen's Room prior to the creation of the Banquet Room. In the first section, where the bedroom used to be, the fresco is by Mengs and it represents *Dawn*. In 1880 the original stuccoes and other scenes of the same painter that were also at the ceiling were destroyed, and they represented *the four moments of the day* around the central scene, because Sabatini's stucco decoration was copied, such as it is in the vault at the other end of the dining room, in order to be symmetrical. Also disappeared the frieze painted in the upper section of the walls by Langlois and Alejandro González Velázquez. Fernando VII had it decorated ostentatiously the "Turkish way" as a "large Queen's private sitting room", with a rich green damask drapery.

The ceremony of the cushion taking over by the Grandee-of-Spain- Ladies was practically identical to that of the male-Grandees, except for the symbol of their rank; to sit down in front of the Queen, while the other ladies remained standing. "The Ladies proceed to the right-hand side (of the Queen) and they have the cushion in front of them in order to sit down when they are told to do so... Her Majesty addresses to the Ladies: *have a seat*, to the Grandees: *put on your hats*...Then the one who has to take the cushion comes in, with her godmother at her right, who leads her by the hand. Two steps after coming in, they curtsy to Her Majesty; another curtsy at the middle of the room, thereupon greeting the Ladies and the Grandees, who have raised to their feet and have taken off their hats once those who are appearing for the ceremony show up at the door. Her Majesty tells the candidate: *thou may sit down*...[after] a brief communication the prospective incumbent stands up, kisses the Royal hand, and again escorted by her godmother, who has appeared to fetch her, bows to Her Majesty, then to the other Ladies, and eventually, she sits down in the first (cushion) of the unassigned... At the end of the event the Ladies stand up and Her Majesty goes along the circle..." Until well on into the XVIIIth century the women in Spain kept sitting on a cushion on the floor, according to the moorish habit, that already had vanished in the XIXth century: "(Laugh bursts thus sometimes), often repressed in respect for the majesty, and caused by the difficulties undergone by some Ladies in sitting down and getting up, and that are incongruous with the solemnity of the ceremony... being necessary to resort to the mutual help that nowadays they give each other..."
Palatial Guide, nr. 12, Madrid, 1898.

The fresco of the central vault that corresponded to the Queen's Chamber is by Antonio González Velázquez and it depicts *Columbus offering the New World to the Catholic Monarchs*, with four chiaroscuro medaillons representing Mexico, Peru, Chile and the Philippines. Fernando VII, in 1818, decided a great decorative campaign with the aim towards turning this Room into the "Great Boudoir" of the new Queen, his second wife Maria Isabel of Braganza: the fundamental pieces, besides the remarkable Empire style furniture and a sumptuous orange silk drapery, were the six pictures painted on chiaroscuro at the pelmets, one of them by Goya, two by Vicente López and the other three by Zacarías G. Velázquez, Aparicio and Camarón. The presence of Goya's work and the feeling as a whole gave this Room an extraordinary importance.

The fresco on the last vault is by Francisco Bayeu, that corresponded to the "third antechamber" or "room for meals and royal audience or levees" of the Queen, and it represents *Boabdil delivering the keys of Granada to the Catholic Monarchs*. It is interesting that, evading the mythological and allegorical field dominating the rest of the vaults of the Palace, History was chosen as the topic on the Queen's Room vaults, turning to Isabella the Catholic Queen's figure, in two of her most outstanding acts, as a reference and an unavoidable model for any Spanish Sovereign. During Fernando VII's reign this room was called the Queen's Oratory, and under Isabel II, when it accomplished an identical rôle for the King consort, the large circular coach which is currently in Carlos III's Anteroom used to be here.

Plateresque Room

Under Carlos III it was the first antechamber of the Queen. When the Banquet Room was carried out, Lema also modified the three rooms located between said eating space and the main courtyard in order to use them as relief, service and transit areas: he knocked down all the partitions and ceilings with which they had been divided into smaller rooms during the reigns of Carlos III's and Carlos IV's, turning them into their original sizes, and he decorated the central one with pilasters and other architectonic elements with motifs from the Spanish "plateresque" art, carved by Manuel Genné. This ornamentation within the liking for the use of historical styles, is very peculiar due to the early use of such local Renaissance repertoire vice the Italian shapes of the Quattrocento. The aim was to gild the background of the carving to make this stand out but finally everything remained in white and even, next to a door, a sample was left as to how the varnished ensemble and the golden carved would have looked. This sudden interruption is explained by Alfonso XII's death in 1885.

In Alfonso XIII's day this Room was used to show of movies to the Royal Family. At the present time stands here an important centerpiece or

Reliquary of the Royal Chapel.

Preliminary sketch for one of the pilasters of the Plateresque Room. José Segundo de Lema, A.G.P.

Florentine *dessert* of the second half of the XVIIIth century, enlarged at the Buen Retiro workshop of hard stones during Carlos IV's reign, and a selection of the most important medals of the collection kept at the Royal Library, in six showcases, from Felipe V to nowadays.

Silver Room

This was the second antechamber of the Queen; like in the preceding and in the following ones, the alterations of Carlos IV and Fernando VII caused the loss of the fresco on the vault, and it was also returned in

Fresco of the vault of the Stradivarius Room: Benignity accompanied by the four cardinal virtues. *Antonio González Veláquez.*

in 1880 to its original dimensions by Lema, who installed the elegant wood and marble baseboard. Currently a selection of the civil silver cutlery used by the Royal Family is here exhibited. Joseph Bonaparte ordered to melt all the former one in order to support the war needs, and thus the very rich Eighteenish royal silverware got lost.

Among those exhibited stand out the ones performed in Martínez's Madrid Silver Factory commissioned by Fernando VII for Queen Maria Isabel of Braganza's Boudoir, in addition to other "Isabelline" and "Alfonsinas" pieces, not specified because the cards explain them plenty well. The religious silverware is in the Reliquary and at the adjacent strongbox of the Royal Chapel, not open to the public currently.

PRINCE DON LUIS' ROOM

The three following halls of the tour were the first of the Room that, since 1764 until his exile from the Court was occupied by Prince don Luis, Carlos III's brother, and from 1785 on by Prince don Gabriel. In Isabel II's reign it was assigned to the Dukes of Montpensier, and in Alfonso XII's and

Viola, violoncello and two violins quartet, Antonio Stradivari.

Alfonso XIII's days to Princess Isabel, "la Chata" (the snub-nosed).

In the first antechamber a selection of the porcelain royal sets of dishes is exhibited. There was a fresco painting here that disappeared due to the Fernando VII's restorations: *The power of Spain in the four areas of the World,* ascribed by Fabre to Luis González Velázquez. During Alfonso XII's reign it was Princess Isabel's Anteroom, and the current ceiling painting by the theatrical designers Busato and Bonardi dates from then.

Antechamber, or Room of the Stradivarius

The *quartet* -viola, violoncello and two violins- here exhibited, was performed by the very famous luthier of Cremona *Antonio Stradivari* for the King of Spain, and purchased by Carlos IV, and another violoncello from the same craftsman. In the middle of the Room, a bronze model of the *monument to Isabella the Catholic Queen,* by Manuel Oms, inaugurated at the Paseo de la Castellana of Madrid in 1883.

The vault keeps the decoration of stucco and painting from Carlos III's period; the fresco represents *Kindness accompanied by the four cardinal virtues* and it is due to one of the González brothers (Antonio according to Ponz and Ceán, or his brother Luis, according to Fabre), Guiaquinto's disciples. In those days this Room was Prince don Luis' dining and Levee room, and from 1785 on of Prince don Gabriel, who placed here the best pictures of his collection. With Fernando VII it was the Queen's dining room, and later on Montpensier's and Princess Isabel's antechamber. The marble flooring comes from Carlos III's period and it was moved from the adjacent room when the Banquet

The people at the Palace.
"Having made our way through the dense crowd that surrounded the entrance [...] As *extranjeros,* we were admitted without waiting for our with the crowd of inodoriferous manolas, and unwashed majos [...] A *alabardero* was assigned to accompany us, at whose appearance a line was inmediately formed, so that we passed in safety up a large stone staircase, and through a passage containing one of the thickest human masses I ever beheld. We at lenght arrived at a narrow door, where the concourse was greater than ever [...] At lenght we arrive at the chamber of death. On a large square four-posted bed lay the Prince of Asturias, embalmed and enclosed in a glass coffin. Guards of the Palace lined the apartment, wearing a handsome uniform, somewhat similar to that of the *Garde Française,* the colours blue, turned up with red, and holding halberts [...] Priests, in magnificent costume, stand near the body of the royal infant [...] but we had not much time to examine the different objects. The Spaniards, crossing themselves, walked on, and we were desired to do the same, to make place for the many persons who desired to see the corpse."
H. Drummond WOLFF: *Madrilenia; or Pictures of the Spanish Life.* London, 1851.

57

Detail of the fresco in Prince don Luis Chamber: The Providence, *Francisco Bayeu.*

Room was created, in 1880, date to which the wallpaper just being replaced also corresponded.

Prince don Luis' Chamber
The vault is admirably painted on fresco by Francisco Bayeu, who gets very close to the qualities of his master Mengs in this work, the best of those that he performed at the.Palace, *Providence presiding man's virtues and faculties.* The wallpaper is new, but it resembles a "Fernandino" model.

Several musical instruments from the XVIIIth and XIXth centuries are here exhibited, among which stand out the vertical pianos which shape imitates the bookshelves, built for Carlos IV by two Franciscos: Fernández (1805) and Flórez (1807). The one performed by the latter is delicately decorated with bronzes, fine woods and painted crystal; two pianos for children, one of them by Lesieur and another by Rodrigo Ten (1918); a few guitars of the beginning of the XIXth century; and two Erard's harps (1861). The Italian *stipo* follows the Florentine models typical of the XVIIth century, but it rather looks to be Milanese of the XIXth century. The huge

Marble and bronze table. Thomire.

Dish with a View of Burgos, *from the landscape set of dishes. Boin.*

table of the sphinxes, designed by Percier and Fontaine, is a work of the bronzesmith Thomire, a gift from Napoleon to Carlos IV. On its board, that is a non-Spanish sample collection of marbles and hard stones, was signed the *Treaty of adherence by Spain to the European Community* in 1985, in the Hall of Columns of this Palace.

The remaining rooms of this flat, that are small and which balconies look out on the Park and the gardens, are not open to the public; they include several ceilings painted on fresco by Gónzalez Velázquez, Maella, Bayeu and others, but among all stands out a charming one painted by Gian Domenico and Lorenzo Tiépolo, with all kind of birds.

Dishes Room

A selection of the most important set of dishes can be admired in this Room: that of Felipe V, from the Indies Company; that of Carlos III, commissioned to Meissen in 1738; and the one of the Princes of Asturias Carlos and Maria Luisa, made in Sèvres in 1776. The abundance of those ordered by Fernando VII and Isabel II to Paris, specially the so-called landscapes set of dishes, from the Parisian

A piece of Felipe V's chinaware. The Indies Company.

The main Courtyard of the Palace.

manufacturers de Boin au Palais Royal, consoles for the loss of many of these Eighteenish pieces.

MAIN GALLERY

The vast corridor that surrounds the courtyard at the level of the main floor allowed to enter the room of each royal person through their respective guard room or antechamber, being therefore the main artery for the circulation of the courtiers; it was also accessible by means of the two general staircases to go up to the upper floors, called of Caceres and of Ladies, that are located at the Northwest and Northeast angles.

The architecture of the gallery is such as it was conceived by Sacchetti, except that according to his project the large windows would have been divided with stone jambs and lintels. Carlos III

"...the superb collection of Flemish tapestry with which the courtyard gallery of the second floor is decorated on the special days...".
A. GERMOND DE LAVIGNE:
*Itineraire descriptif, historique et littéraire de Madrid...*Paris, 1859.

The Emperor Theodosius, *Giandomenico Olivieri.*

Main gallery.

"Here [at the main floor] is a second colonnade and gallery, which looks upon the court, and which is paved with marble. This is always filled with groups of body guards and halberdiers on service, and with people in court dresses ready to go before the sovereign."
Alexander Slidell MACKENZIE: *A year in Spain, by a young American.* London, 1831.

"The doors of a coved ante-chamber flew open, and after passing through an enfilade of saloons peopled with ladies-in-waiting and pages (some mere children), we entered a lofty chamber hung with white satin, formed into compartments by a rich embroidery of gold and colours, and illuminated by a lustre of rock crystal."
William BECKFORD: *Italy; with sketches of Spain and Portugal...* (1787) London, 1834.

ordered Sabatini to simply close them with large iron frames such as we see them now. He further ordered not to place the series in relief of political, military, scientific and religious range of topics that Father Sarmiento had disposed to place at the frames of multiple lines adorning the windows; those that did get performed are nowadays at the Prado Museum and deposited at the San Fernando Academy.

Through any of the large windows we can watch the noble architecture of the courtyard, square, lightly displaced to the North within the Palace frame, since the architect conceived from the

Royal Chapel: The Crowning of the Virgin *and other paintings of sacred topics. Corrado Giaquinto.*

"The chapel-royal is a gem of decoration, and rich in paintings and valuable marbles [...] the effect of the *tout ensemble* is gorgeous... Visitors are admitted by tickets to the high mass on Sundays [...] The appointed hour was twelve o'clock, and we were puntual to the time. We found the portion of the chapel reserved for strangers very crowded; but though there were many foreigners as usual, our party were the only representatives of our country. The grand staircase was thrown open, and the corridor, along which the royal family were to pass from the state chambers into the chapel, was carpeted [...] The sentinels walked up and down with the most solemn air, and two *Suisses,* or *celadores,* strutted about the entrance with most pavonic importance. The Chapel was carpeted, but in much more respectable style, and a really gorgeous daïs, and canopy, covered with cloth of gold, were prepared for the Queen and King Consort, with the royal arms embroidered in rich colours on the back; two thrones, with footstools and *prie-dieux* before them, stood on the daïs."
Mrs. William PITT BYRNE: *Things of Spain. Illustrative of Spain and the Spaniards as they are.* London, 1866.

"As the king was staying at the palace [...] we could not see the rooms; but had to content ourselves with looking at His Majesty's private chapel, where a service was going on. The organ is very superior to the generality of Spanish instruments, and occasionally delivered itself of very striking sounds". Zouch Horace TURTON: *To the desert and back; or, Travels in Spain, the Barbary States, Italy, etcetera, in 1875-1876.* London, 1876.

beginning the southern corridor to be wider with the aim of housing the main staircase and the Chapel, that in the old Alcazar lay between the two courtyards of the King and the Queen. In order to emphasize the axis of the main entrance Sacchetti built wider the central arches of the South and of the North sides, at the expense of narrowing the collateral ones, where the four statues of the Roman emperors are placed that Carlos III had removed from below the large balcony of the façade; Sabatini placed them here in 1791.

In the great ceremonies the gallery was carpeted and the wall facings were covered with tapestries of the Royal Collection, so that the access to the Chapel appeared to be more impressive.

ROYAL CHAPEL

Sculptures of each of the Catholic Monarchs, by Ponciano Ponzano, flank the door of the Royal Chapel. In 1742, due to Scotti's critical remarks, it was decided not to locate the Chapel where it was originally contemplated, i.e., where is now the Halberdiers Hall, but in its current site by eliminating several of the Princes Rooms. After planning several options, and always tending to make them larger, Sacchetti formulated in 1748 his definitive plan, according to which it was built just as it is now. Nevertheless, the decoration, never did get finished pursuant to the architect's ideas, who had planned to do both the flooring and the covering

Royal Chapel. Canopy or canopied throne.

Royal Chapel, Annunciation altar. Antonio Rafael Mengs.

of all the walls with marble, and further with bronze the capitals and the columns and pilasters bases. Also, neither the altarpieces, nor the shape of the glass partition - that is the glazed tribune at the foot of the chapel, destined to the Kings - nor that of the choir follow Sacchetti's final proposal: Carlos III ordered to complete everything on stucco "provisionally" as it still looks nowadays, since he planned to amplify the Chapel by adding a projection towards the North, and in that sense Sabatini made two projects; that never were carried out fortunately.

"Everything about the Madrid Alcazar is grand, if not strictly beautiful [...] a stately entrance to the somewhat too gorgeous suite of state apartments; everything on a large scale, and befitting a grand Imperial home."
Antonio C.N. GALLENGA: *Iberian reminiscences. Fifteen years' travelling impressions of Spain and Portugal.* London 1883.

Terrace overlooking the main Courtyard

The decoration proposed by Sacchetti, with Ventura Rodríguez' and Corrado Giaquinto's collaboration, if it ever had been completed, would have constituted a magnificence hard to beat. Of said decoration were performed the whole ornamentation of the vaults and the ten large columns of black marble of Mañaria (Basque Country), of a single piece.

From the cornice upwards, everything is by Giaquinto: his are the designs of the stuccos, performed by Andrioli, and again his are the grandiose frescoes representing *St. James at Clavijo* above the entrance, *The Glory* with *the Holy Trinity crowning The Virgin* at the dome, and in its pendentives the saints *Leandre, Damaso, Isidore the Plowman and Saint Mary of the Head*; *The Trinity* in the gallery that is behind the altar - since it was planned to locate it further back - and, in the choir *Allegory of the Religion*. The cherubim are by Felipe de Castro, except for the ones flanking the eucharistical symbol that are by Olivieri.

In comparison with the sumptuous group of the vaults the picture of the high altar is very modest, *St. Michael* by Francisco Bayeu following an original by Giordano and a drawing by his master Mengs, to whom *The Annunciation* is due, that is his last work, unfinished at his death in Rome in 1779. The architecture of both altarpieces is by Sabatini, except for the table of the latter, due to Isidro Velázqez, and where the relics of the Roman martyr saint Felix are resting. The Holy Hearts sculptures are of Juan Samsó, and those of the Four Evangelists in the José Ginés antechapel.

Besides the daily cult officiated by a large staff of chaplains, who were commanded by the cardinal Patriarch of the Indies, almoner and His Majesty's master pro-chaplain, the solemn ceremonies displayed a great pomp. Generally the King, as well as the other royal people, used to follow the rite from the glass partition or glazed tribune at the foot of the chapel that were reached through the interior of the royal rooms, but in the solemn festivities he would come out in procession by the gallery of the courtyard decked out with tapestries; upon reaching the Chapel he would bow before the altar, and then again before the Queen who was standing at the glass partition, thereafter occupying his seat of honor in the curtain, or canopy. Every Court member had a place assigned: right next to the King were the Mayor of the Palace and the Captain of the Royal Guard. Thereafter the Grandees facing the door, etc. The public was only allowed to occupy the entrance section, or antechapel.

Fernando VI wanted a sumptuous Chapel, although it was not very large, so he endeavored for that aim in all the details, including even the liturgical vestments - very numerous, but the *pontifical* named after him is worth to mention -, the choir books and the organ, since music meant a lot to that Monarch, as it had to his father, and the Royal Chapel had a numerous and selected group of instrumentalists and voices. The organ, which box was designed by Ventura Rodríguez, began with Leonardo Fernández Dávila and was finished by the Majorcan Jorge Bosch. It is

Royal Chapel. High altar and royal canopy.

unique in Spain not only due to its intrinsical quality, but also because it escaped from any Nineteenth-century restorations. It has just now been subject of a scrupulous restoration job.

QUEEN MARIA LUISA' BACK ROOM.

Alfonso XII's Billiards Room
The main gallery leads to the first of Maria Luisa of Parma's back rooms. Thus were called at the Palace the rooms of the royal

Design for the Billiards Room, José Segundo de Lema. A.G.P.

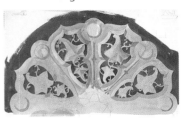

Billiards Room.

Magnificence.
"The first view of the exterior conveys an idea of magnifincence ... The interior of the building compensates for the external faults, being excelled by no palace in Europe in splendour and elegance... Those [the apartments] of the Queen, which we next entered, are on a much grander scale, extending the whole lenght of the palace, and communicating with each other, so that when the folding doors are thrown open, the eye is almost dazzled by the splendid elegance of a long suite of magnificent saloons [...] In short, every thing is so magnificent, as to shut out all idea of comfort: the eye is dazzled, the mind struck with admiration, but neither is pleased. For my own part, the reflection I made was, how miserable I should be if forced to inhabit these superb apartments! for I am so unambitious as to prefer a well polished snug mahogany table, a good fire, and the society of a few friends, to grandeur accompanied by ceremony and formality, which must have been always the case here; as none ever entered these apartments but in full dress, and with a feeling of their own inferiority".
Andrew Thomas, lord BLAYNEY: *Narrative of a forced journey through Spain and France as a prisoner of war in the years 1810 to 1814.*

quarters that did not face towards the façades, they were interiors or they received light from the courtyard, and they were kept for relaxing and the privacy off the Court life routine. The vault of this Room is painted in fresco by Mariano Salvador Maella in 1769, with a mythological scene, *June ordering Aeolus to free the winds against Aeneas.* This is no doubt the best ever done in this genre by this painter young in those days and who later on was too generous, but it is hidden by the wood coffered ceiling that J.S. de Lema designed when in 1879 Alfonso XII had him built here a Billiards Room: following English Victorian examples and the Rationalist derivation that Viollet-le-Duc performed with Gothic motifs, Lema carried out a work characteristic of his style and of the taste in those years, very coherent and not without charm, finished in 1881 and restored in 1993. The joint and the carving of the mahogany panelling are due to Antonio Girón, like the rest of the furniture except for the table, that is Parisian.

Alfonso XII's Smoking Room.

Near to the Billiards Room said King wanted a smoking room decorated à la "Chinese". Lema covered the walls with porcelain plates ordered to the Boulanger Factory, in Choisy-le-Roi (Paris) and with embroidered silk fabrics, as they look nowadays after the 1993 restoration, since the ensemble had been stripped down after 1939 due to damages in the Civil War bombing. However, the decision was made to not replace the ceiling, that was also ornamented in the same fashion, to leave the Eighteenish century style of the stucco ornament visible and Joaquín Espalter's painting in tempera, dating from 1857.

Queen Maria Luisa's plaster Private Sitting Room.

In spite of its small dimensions, this neoclassic private sitting room is one of the most fascinating rooms of the Palace. It was designed by Francisco Sabatini and carried out by the stucco plasterers the Brilli brothers, who found inspiration in the Pompeii archaeological repertoire then in vogue.

Smoking or Japanese Room, detail.

Design for the Smoking Room, José Segundo de Lema. A.G.P.

Plaster Private Sitting Room, detail.

Plaster Private Sitting Room.

Queen Maria Luisa's fine woods Private Sitting Room.

In an obvious contrast with the foregoing room, this rococo taste private Sitting Room, and its pieces of furniture - a bureau, two chests of drawers, an armchair and two ceremonial chairs - were made by a team of cabinetmakers and bronzesmiths managed by Gasparini; it seems to be one of the private sitting rooms of Carlos III, removed

from its original place and adapted here in Carlos IV's time: although the taste was already very old-fashioned the sumptuousness of the work was worthy of the Queen; the design of the flooring and the stuccoes of the ceiling are due to J.B. Ferroni.

Private fine woods sitting-room of Queen Maria Luisa.

The rooms not open to the public. The Royal Library.
Queen Maria Luisa's and Carlos IV's Rooms.

To these *back rooms* corresponds, logically, the Queen's Room, the balconies of which room overlook the Orient Square. Thereafter, Carlos IV rooms also overlooked this Square and the Parade Square. Of all these halls, not open to the public, due to the frequent use of His Majesty the King for his military and civil audiences and other official events, are worth mentioning: *doña Maria Cristina's Anteroom*, with Carlos IV's furniture; the *Daily Dining Room*, with Sabatini's architectonic decoration; *Queen Maria Luisa's Boudoir*, called the Mirrors Hall, an exquisite work from the same architect and from the same stucco plasterers as the small plaster Private Sitting Room; the *Tapestry Room*, called so for those of Joseph's, David's and Solomon's history that decorate it; that of *Arms*, with XVIth century

Panel of Florentine mosaic in the rooms that belonged to the Queen Maria Luisa.

Frieze of the private fine woods sitting room of Queen Maria Luisa. Detail.

"This palace, whether it be viewed with reference to its architecture or decoration, is, indeed, a noble one. I have heard it said, by those who had visited the chief capitals of Europe, that they had seen none superior to it, and, though Versailles may excel in detail, as a perfect whole the palace of Madrid may even claim pre-eminence."
Alexander Slidell MACKENZIE: *A year in Spain, by a young American.* London 1831.

tapestries; the *Chamber*, with large Carlos III's console tables. The vaults of all these rooms are painted in fresco by F. Bayeu and M. S. Maella, that of the *Antechamber* by Gian Domenico Tiépolo, and that of the *Anteroom* by Gian Battista Tiépolo.

Former Carlos IV Library, later on private rooms of the Kings in the XIXth and XXth centuries.

For the same reasons are not open to the public neither the rooms which the St. Gil wing houses - between the Parade Square and Bailén St. - with access through Carlos IV's Chamber and where this King had his Library, and Isabel II, and afterwards her successors, their private rooms. Their ceilings shape a very united group of stuccoes and paintings performed between 1784 and 1787, the former according to Sabatini's designs and the latter by Bayeu and Maella. The decoration and the furniture correspond to the last period when these rooms

Mirror with Carlos III's effigy, *carried out at the Crystal Royal Factory of San Ildefonso about 1775, according to a portrait, by Antonio Rafael Mengs. Royal Library.*

Of how the Palace, without growing, becomes large.

"When the Bourbons were reigning the whole Royal Palace was occupied: the King inhabited on the left-hand side, towards the Orient Square; doña Isabel II the section that overlooks on a side the Orient Square and on the other the Parade Square; Montpensier the side opposite to that of the Queen; the Princes had each one a lodging towards the Campo del Moro gardens. [*It was on the contrary: the King consort in Carlos III's rooms and those of the western façade, currently the Banquet Room; and the Princesses, in the eastern rooms: The wing of Isabel II's private rooms was also the one occupied later on by Alfonso XIII*].

During the time that King Amadeo was around, a great part of the building remained empty. It had only three small rooms: a study, an alcove and the boudoir. The alcove faced to a long corridor that led to the Princes' rooms, next to the Queen's room, who never wanted to be far from her children. There was also a room for receptions. All this section that served for the whole Royal Family was formerly occupied just by Queen Isabel. When she found out that don Amadeo and doña Victoria were satisfied with such a small space, it is told that she said completely amazed: the poor youngsters, they could not possibly move!"

Edmond of AMICIS: *Spain. Travel during Amadeus I's reign.* Florence, 1872.

were lived in, Alfonso XIII's reign, but it integrates very interesting pieces from an earlier time. French and Spanish furniture from the XVIIIth century are remarkable, a fine woods suite of furniture by Gasparini and "Fernandino" chandeliers.

The Royal Library
The private Royal Library or of His Majesty Chamber, as it was called in the XVIIIth century, is not included in the tourist tour. It is located on the first floor since Maria Cristina of Bourbon had it moved from the main floor to occupy its halls with the private rooms; its halls, with

Mirrors Hall, that was Queen Maria Luisa of Parma's Boudoir. Ornamental stuccoes. José and Domingo Brilli, under Francisco Sabatini's management.

bookshelves of Isabel II's and Alfonso XII's time, have a lot of class, and the founds of manuscripts and of ancient printed items are very important, in addition to the wealth of the illuminated manuscripts and of the binders that it keeps. It offers to the investigators an excellent working spot in the mornings.

Main vestibule, with Carlos III's statue in front of the staircase. Pedro Michel

THE FIRST OR GROUND FLOOR

Main Vestibule. Detail.

The main vestibule, where the gift-shop is located, leads to the Carlos III's petty room for the royal guard: the opposite large door is that of the rooms that since 1924 are called "of Genoa". During the Ancient Régime the State Ministry was there located; the Ministries of War and Navy stood nearby, following the gallery of the main courtyard, at which back was the so called Ministry of Grace and Justice - at the place where the Library is now located -: furthermore the Indies Ministry, at the end of the other gallery parallel to this one, that starts from the Main Stewardship Hall, that is the one at the opposite side of the main hall. Finally, the entrance to the Treasury Ministry was by the current access to the National Heritage

Round shield of The Medusa. *Royal Armory.*

"The distant hills beyond the river have a wild, uncultivated, but rather grand appearance; and in the distance, the fine range of the Guadarrama, covered with snow, is such a view as is certainly not enjoyed from a royal palace in any other metropolis; and fortunately it is not spoilt by any straggling, ugly suburbs."
G.A. HOSKINS: *Spain, as it is.* London, 1851.

Equestrian armor of Carlos V.

quarters by the Parade Square. Thus this floor lodged the most essential activity of the administration of the vast Spanish Monarchy at the moment of its maximum territorial area.

Leaving towards the Parade Square and taking the arches gallery that passes by the gate of the *Palace General Archive*, -the most important of Madrid second only to The National Historic Archive - and that overlooks the landscape spread as far as the Sierra, the Royal Armory is reached.

ROYAL ARMORY

It is the most important in Europe along with the Vienna Imperial Armory, based both upon the merit of its pieces and the history that confers a sense to such an Arms Collection, mainly in the luxury field. Felipe II had moved it over here and to place it at the building that bore this name and it was standing where there is now the closing gate.

The current pavilion, that houses a large hall, was designed by the architects J.S. de Lema and E. Repullés, and it was inaugurated in 1897. The Collection is open to the public for over four centuries. The existence of a specific guide about this treasure relieves us from offering any further information in this regard.

Main façade of the Palace. An axis with one of the doors leading to the small vestibules.

"It appeared to me a much handsomer building than the Tuilleries. One always looks upon it with renewed pleasure; for it leaves upon the mind that impression of gracefulness combined with strength, which are the essential attributes of beauty."
Michael Joseph QUINN: *A visit to Spain...in the latter part of 1822 and the first months of 1823.*

Royal Pharmacy. Baroque Herbarium.

THE ROYAL PHARMACY

The pavilion at the other side of the Parade Square houses the Royal Pharmacy Office, that used to supply drugs to the Royal Family and all the employees and staff of the Royal House. At the entrance and at the

The Palace from the Orient Square.
Equestrian statue of Felipe IV.
Pietro Tacca.

The Palace as a labyrinth.
"It is composed of three stories under-
ground, and five above-ground. The
rooms (or cellars) of the lower story
under ground ... [are] to serve as a
repository of the eatables. The kitchens
will take up the story over it; and over
the kitchens all the people employed
in them will be lodged. Those three
stories are so well contrived, that even
the lowermost is not totally deprived
of light ... If the undergroun
apartments are grand, you may easily
think that those above-ground cannot
be mean. Those on the ground-floor
are already inhabited by some of the
great officers at court. The King's
apartments are over those ot the great
officers... and the fourth and fifth
occupied by their attendants."
Joseph BARETTI: *Journey from London
to Genoa, through England, Portugal,
Spain and France* (in 1760). London,
1770.

*Royal Pharmacy. A piece of the
set of pots.*

corridor there are several XVIIIth century glazed earthenware jars or vessels
from Talavera. In the first room at the right-hand side have been placed the
sets of pots and the shelves coming from the pharmacy of the former
General Hospital of Madrid, going back to the end of the XVIIIth century.
Thereafter comes the second room, containing sets of pots of the Royal
Pharmacy from the XVIIIth century; the third room, with Nineteenish sets of
porcelain pots; then comes the fourth room, with La Granja crystal jars, also
from the XIXth century. The last room shows a reconstruction intent of an
antique pharmaceutical "office".

AROUND THE PALACE

THE EXTERIOR OF THE ROYAL PALACE. THE ORIENT SQUARE. THE SABATINI GARDENS. THE GARDENS OF THE PARK OR "CAMPO DEL MORO" (MOOR'S FIELD)

The Parade Square, inserted between the iron gate and the New Cathedral, is narrow and therefore it does not offer a perspective of the Royal Palace as distant and impressive as it would have happened in the event that under Alfonso XII the idea of building in this site - meant to become a forecourt of arms since Sacchetti's time - the Almudena Temple, ended in 1992, would not have succeeded.

To enjoy the admirable aspect that the Palace offers from faraway it is necessary to go, therefore, to the Orient Square, a space built by Joseph Napoleon by knocking down several buildings of the Royal

The Palace from the Bailén Street with the Sabatini Gardens.

House, and definitely urbanized and landscaped under Isabel II, when at its center the monument with the magnificent *Equestrian Statue of Felipe IV* was placed, a work of the Florentine Pietro Tacca, opposite the Prince's Gate at the Palace.

From Bailén St., an outside staircase goes down to the *Gardens*, created during the Second Republic at the site of the *Royal Stables* that following Carlos III's orders his architect *Sabatini* built here, and that are named after him. The northern façade of the Palace displays here all the height of its floors and the Royal Chapel dome.

From these Gardens, a ramp goes down to San Vicente Boulevard and bordering the iron gate as far as the one of the Virgen del Puerto, the entrance to the Palace Park, commonly called Moor's Field is reached. This historical Park, created under Felipe II, is very pleasant although the actual installation is less interesting than the potential one, since in the XVIIIth century several projects were planned among which those of Sacchetti, Ventura Rodríguez, plus the one commissioned in 1747 to Esteban Boutelou - chief gardener at Aranjuez - and Garnier de L'Isle - Versailles supervisor - are specially noteworthy; but neither one of them was ever performed, nor Sabatini's (1767), but it was necessary to wait to Isabel II's reign, when that of Narciso Pascual y Colomer (1844) was begun, of which the design of the main rectilinear avenues still subsists, and the two fountains lined up in the central axis: that of the *Shells*, a work of Felipe de Castro and Manuel Álvarez (1775), proceeding from the palace of the Prince don Luis at Boadilla del Monte, and that of the *Tritones*, an Italian job of the XVIth century, coming from the Islet Garden of Aranjuez, and located before the "large grotto" or greenhouse. Finally, during Maria Cristina of Hapsburg's regency, the park was totally modified according to the pseudo-landscape design of Ramón Oliva (1890).

The splendid view that Sacchetti's building offers from the central avenue of the Garden invites us to look after its most spectacular aspect from a more remote point, from the ancient royal properties of the *Casa de Campo* or from the Prince Pío Hill, it is, indeed, from this perspective as it is possible to understand this Royal Palace.

The Palace from the Park or "Campo del Moro", with the fountain of the Shells.

The Palace in the Madrid landscape.

"Seen from the old Castile road, from the Manzanares banks, from the North Station or from the Príncipe Pío Hill, this Palace has an imposing look, raised on the big containing walls and buttresses, the terraces and the gardens in slope shaping a magnificent pedestal, and with its white bulk silhouetted against this beautiful sky in such a peculiar way...".
A. GERMOND DE LAVIGNE: *Itineraire descriptif, historique et littéraire de Madrid...* Paris, 1859.

"The Royal Palace, of an architecture both rich and severe, turns two of its four faces towards the countryside, so that it becomes necessary to descend quite uneasily down to the bottom of a kind of abyss in order to be able to watch the most notable of the façades, in case you try to realize its position; the main façade is in front of a large square where no important road runs into; the fourth and last of its sides is the only one that can be seen from the Orient Square, and even there the perspective cannot be enjoyed once one walks into one of the adjoining streets".
Marie Studolmine RATAZZI: *L'Espagne moderne*. Paris, 1879.

"The Palace of Madrid is a splendid building [...] The east front is very handsome and imposing, and the west side is also magnificent; a noble and very extensive inclined drive, reminding me in form of the approach to the Monte Pincio, in Rome, leads up to a noble terrace before the Palace."
HOSKINS, G.A. *Spain, as it is*. London, 1851.

79

BIBLIOGRAPHY

Alcázar of Madrid

ORSO, Steven N.: *In the presence of the Planet King: Philip IV and the decoration of the Alcázar of Madrid.* Princeton University Press 1986 (revisión de tesis, doctoral, 1978).

GERARD, Véronique: *De castillo a Palacio. El Alcázar de Madrid en el siglo XVI.* Madrid, Xarait, 1984 (recoge la bibliografía anterior).

BARBEITO, José: *El Alcázar de Madrid.* Tesis doctoral defendida en la Escuela de Arquitectura, Universidad Politécnica de Madrid, 1988. Publicada por el C.O.A.M., Madrid 1992.

AA.VV.: *El Real Alcázar de Madrid.* Catálogo de la exposición, a cargo de Fernando Checa Cremades. Comunidad de Madrid, 1994.

Guide books

NIÑO MAS, Felipe, y JUNQUERA DE VEGA, Paulina: *Guía ilustrada del Palacio Real de Madrid*, Patrimonio Nacional. Madrid, 1956, 3.ª ed. De esta guía existen ediciones corregidas y aumentadas en 1966, por M. López Serrano, y en 1985, por F. Fernández-Miranda y Lozana.

General

AGUEDA VILLAR, Mercedes: *Antonio Rafael Mengs 1728-1799.* Catalogo exposición, Museo del Prado, Madrid, 1980.

ANDRADA, Ramón: "Las estatuas del Palacio de Oriente vuelven a su sitio", *R.S.*, 1972, 9, n° 31, pp. 49-56.

ANDRADA, Ramón: "Obras de reconstrucción en el Palacio de Oriente", *R.S.*, 1965, 2, n° 3, pp. 70-75.

Apollo, LXXXVI, n° 75, Londres, mayo 1968: monográfico sobre el Palacio Real de Madrid.

BARRENO SEVILLANO, Mª Luisa: "Pontifical bordado. Capilla del Palacio Real de Madrid", *R.S.*, 1978, 15, N° 56, PP. 17-28.

BARRENO SEVILLANO, Mª Luisa: "Salón de Gasparini o pieza de la parada", *R.S.*, 1975, 12, n° 43, pp. 61-72.

BENITO GARCIA, Pilar: "Los textiles y el mobiliario del Palacio Real de Madrid", *R.S.*, 1991, 28, N° 109, pp. 45-60.

BOTTINEAU, Yves: *L'Art de Cour dans l'Espagne de Philipe V*, Burdeos 1962. Ed. esp., *El arte cortesano en la España de Felipe V (1700-1746)*, Madrid, F.U.E., 1986. Nueva edición francesa, corregida y aumentada, Societé des amis du Musée de Sceaux, Paris 1992.

BOTTINEAU, Yves: *L' Art de Cour dans l'Espagne des Lumières*, Paris, De Boccard, 1986.

CABEZA GIL-CASARES, Carmen: "Bordados del salón de Gasparini", *R.S.*, 1992, 29, N° 114, pp. 12-28.

CABEZA GIL-CASARES, Carmen, y SANCHO, José Luis: "La restauración de las salas de billar y de fumar en el P.R.M., la recuperación de un conjunto alfonsino", en *R.S.*, N° 118 (1993).

CHECA CREMADES, Fernando: "Los frescos del Palacio Real Nuevo de Madrid y el fin del lenguaje alegórico", *Archivo Español de Arte*, LXV, 258 (1992), pp. 157-178, con bibliografía completa y puesta al día.

COLON DE CARVAJAL, José Ramón: *Catálogo de Relojes del Patrimonio Nacional.* P.N., Madrid 1987.

CUMBERLAND, R., *An accurate and descriptive Catalogue of the several paintings in the King of Spain 's Palace at Madrid*, Londres, 1787.

DURAN SALGADO, Miguel: *Exposición de proyectos*

no realizados relativos al Palacio de Oriente y sus jardines. Madrid, 1935.

ECHALECU, J. Mª, "Los talleres reales de ebanistería, bronces y bordados", *Archivo Español de Arte*. 1955, tomo XXVIII, pags. 237-259.

ESPOZ Y MINA, Condesa de (Juana Vega de Mina): *Apuntes para la historia del tiempo en que ocupó los destinos de aya de S.M. y A. y camarera mayor de Palacio su autora —*. Madrid 1910.

FABRE, Francisco José: *Descripcion de las Alegorías pintadas en las bóvedas del Real Palacio de Madrid, hecha de orden de S.M. por...*, Madrid, Aguado, 1829.

FEDUCHI, Luis M: *Colecciones reales de España: el mueble*. Patrimonio Nacional, Madrid 1965.

FEDUCHI, Luis M.: *El mueble en España. Volúmenes I y II: El Palacio Nacional*. Madrid, Afrodisio Aguado, 1949.

GARCIA MERCADAL, J., *Viajes de extranjeros por*

España y Por-tugal. Recopilación, traducción, prologo y notas por — Aguilar, Madrid, 1962.

GOMEZ MOLINERO, Encarnación, y SANCHEZ HERNANDEZ, Leticia: "El botamen de cristal de la Real Farmacia. Nuevos datos para SU estudio", *R.S.*, 1987, 24, nº 93, pp. 33-36.

GOMEZ DE LAS HERAS, *El Palacio Real de Madrid*, Madrid 1935.

GRITELLA, Gianfranco: *Juvarra. L'Architettura*. Módena, 1992, vol. II, ficha 124.

IGLESIAS, Helena (dir.): *El Palacio Real de Madrid: un recorrido a través de su arquitectura*. Dibujos de los alumnos de la II Cátedra de Análisis de Formas Arquitectónicas de la ETSAM. Patrimonio Nacional, 1990.

JUNQUERA, Juan José: *La decoración y el mobiliario en los palacios de Carlos IV*. Madrid, 1979.

JUNQUERA, Paulina: "Los libros de coro de la Real Capilla", *R.S.*, 1965, 2, nº 6, pp. 12-27.

JUNQUERA, Paulina: "Muebles franceses con porcelanas en el Palacio de Oriente", *R.S.*, 1966, 3, nº 8, pp. 28-37.

JUNQUERA DE VEGA, Paulina, y HERRERO CARRETERO, Concha: *Catálogo de tapices del Patrimonio Nacional*. Vol. I: siglo XVI. P.N., Madrid 1986.

JUNQUERA DE VEGA, Paulina, y DIAZ GALLEGOS, Carmen: *Catálogo de tapices del Patrimonio Nacional*. Vol. II: siglo XVII. P.N., Madrid 1986.

LOPEZ SERRANO, Matilde (ed.): *El palacio Real de Madrid*, Patrimonio Nacional, Madrid, 1975.

MARTIN, Fernando A.: *Catálogo de la plata del Patrimonio Nacional*. P.N., Madrid 1987

MORALES Y MARIN, José Luis: *Mariano Salvador Maella*, Madrid 1992.

MORALES Y MARIN, José Luis: *Vicente Lopez (1772-1850)*, Cat. expo. Madrid, 1990.

MORALES Y MARIN José Luis: *Los Bayeu*, Zaragoza, 1979.

MORAN TURINA, Juan Miguel: *La imagen del Rey. Felipe V y el arte*, Madrid, 1990.

PEREZ VILLAAMIL, M., *Artes e industrias del Buen Retiro*. Madrid, 1904.

PEREZ GALDOS, Benito: *La de Bringas*. Madrid, 1884. Ed. Hernando, Madrid.

PLAZA SANTIAGO, Francisco Javier de la: *Investigaciones sobre el Palacio Real Nuevo de*

Madrid, Valladolid 1975. Constituye por el momento la monografía fundamental. Recoge toda la bibliografía anterior.

PONZ, Antonio: *Viaje de España*, XVIII tomos, Madrid, 1769-1793. Tomo sexto. Tercera impresión, Madrid, Ibarra 1793.

REYERO, Carlos: "Isabel II y la pintura de historia", *R.S.*, 1991, 28, nº 107, pp. 28-36.

RUIZ ALCON, Mª Teresa: "Habitaciones y objetos personales del rey don Alfonso XIII en el museo del Palacio Real de Madrid", *R.S.*, 1980, 17, Nº 63, PP. 17-28.

SANCHEZ HERNANDEZ, Leticia: "La vajilla de paisajes del Patrimonio Nacional conservada en el Palacio Real de Madrid", *R.S.*, 1985, 22, nº 83, pp. 37-52.

SANCHEZ HERNANDEZ, Mª Leticia: *Catálogo de porcelana y cerámica española del Patrimonio Nacional en los Palacios Reales*. P.N., Madrid 1989.

SANCHO, José Luis: "Sacchetti y los salones del Palacio Real de Madrid", *R.S.*, 1988, 25, nº 96, pp. 37-44.

SANCHO, José Luis: "Proyectos del siglo XVIII para los jardines del Palacio de Madrid: Esteban Boutelou y Garnier de l'Isle", *Anales del Instituto de Estudios Madrileños*, tomo XXV (1988), pp. 403-433.

SANCHO, José Luis: "El Palacio Real de Madrid. Alternativas y críticas a un proyecto". *Reales Sitios*, nº extraordinario (1989), pp. 167-180.

SANCHO, José Luis: "El piso principal del Palacio Real", *Reales Sitios*, nº 109 (1991).

SANCHO, José Luis: "Fernando Fuga, Nicola Salvi y Luigi Vanvitelli; el Palacio Real de Madrid y sus escaleras principales", en *Storia dell'Arte*, Roma, nº 72 (1991), pp. 199-252.

SANCHO, José Luis: "Las críticas en España y desde Italia al Palacio Real de Madrid", *Archivo Español de Arte*, nº 254 (1991), pp. 201-254.

SANCHO, José Luis: "Espacios para la Majestad en el siglo XVIII: la distribución de las habitaciones reales en el Palacio Nuevo de Madrid". *Anales del Instituto de Estudios Madrileños*, tomo XXXI, Madrid 1992, pp. 19-40.

SANCHO, Jose Luis: "Francisco Sabatini, **primer arquitecto**, director de la decoración interior de los palacios reales", artículo en pp. 143-166; y fichas sobre la decoración interior, pp. 227-236, pp. 236-240, pp. 241-244; todo ello en AA.VV.: *Francisco Sabatini, la arquitectura como metáfora del poder*, catálogo de la exposición, Madrid 1993.

SANCHO, José Luis: *La arquitectura de los Sitios Reales. Catálogo histórico de los Palacios, jardines y Patronatos Reales del Patrimonio Nacional*. Patrimonio Nacional-Fundación Tabacalera, Madrid 1995. Con completa bibliografía y planimetría.

TARRAGA BALDO, Mª Luisa: *G. D. Olivieri y el taller de escultura del Palacio Real*. Patrimonio Nacional, C.S.I.C. e Instituto Italiano de Cultura, Madrid, 1992.

TORMO 1927: TORMO, Elías: *Las iglesias del antiguo Madrid*. Madrid, 1927. Reeditado por el Instituto de España. Madrid 1972.

TURMO, Isabel: *Museo de carruajes*. Patrimonio Nacional, 1969.

R.S.: *Reales Sitios*, revista del Patrimonio Nacional.

THE PRINTING OF THIS BOOK, PUBLISHED JOINTLY BY THE PATRIMONIO NACIONAL AND ALDEASA,

WAS FINISHED ON THE 16TH DAY OF AUGUST, 1996 FESTIVITY OF SAN ROQUE

AT T.F. ARTES GRÁFICAS, MADRID.